EXPLORING COMPREHENSION SKILLS

INTRODUCTION

Teachers are under increasing pressure to ensure that their students are successful readers. The *Reading Next** report lists fifteen elements for improving literacy. *Exploring Comprehension Skills* incorporates several of these elements.

◆ **Direct, explicit comprehension instruction** . . . in the strategies and processes that proficient readers use to understand what they read

◆ **Effective instructional principles embedded in context** . . . providing instruction and practice in reading and writing skills specific to . . . content area

◆ **Motivation and self-directed learning** . . . providing students with the instruction and supports needed for independent learning tasks

◆ **Strategic tutoring**, which provides students with intense individualized reading, writing, and content instruction

◆ **Diverse texts** . . . at a variety of difficulty levels and on a variety of topics

Exploring Comprehension Skills provides instruction to help meet the needs of many students. The selections in this book cover a wide range of subjects in areas such as science, social studies, history, sports, and the arts. The high-interest fiction and nonfiction texts with low readability levels encourage readers to focus on skill development instead of reading obstructions.

ORGANIZATION

Exploring Comprehension Skills focuses on six of the most important reading comprehension skills: finding facts, recognizing sequence, understanding context, identifying main ideas, drawing conclusions, and making inferences.

◆ **Facts** Literal comprehension is a foundation skill for understanding a reading selection. Students using the Facts unit practice identifying pieces of information presented in each reading selection. The focus is on specific details that tell who, what, where, when, why, and how.

A facts lesson consists of a reading selection about a single topic broken into two parts. Each part is followed by four questions that require students to find the facts in the selection.

◆ **Sequence** Sequence involves the time order of events and the temporal relationship of one event or step to other events or steps. Reading for sequence means identifying the order of events in a story or the steps in a process.

A sequence lesson consists of a reading selection about a single topic, followed by four questions. The first question asks students to put statements in order based on the information in each selection. The following questions ask about the stated or implied sequence in each selection.

◆ **Context** When students practice using context, they must use all the words in a reading selection to understand the unfamiliar words. As they develop this skill, students become aware of the relationships among words, phrases, and sentences. The skill provides them with a tool to help them understand words and concepts by learning how language is used to express meaning. Mastering this skill allows students to become independent readers.

A context lesson consists of four reading selections. In lessons 1 through 8, the selections are presented in a cloze format with one or two missing words. In lessons 9 through 16, the selections contain a word in boldface type. Students are asked to use the context of the selection to choose the correct definition for each boldfaced word.

◆ **Main Idea** When students read for the main idea, they must read to recognize the overall point made in the reading selection. Students must be able to differentiate the details from the main idea. They must understand the one idea that is supported by all the details in a selection, chapter, or paragraph. Identifying the main idea involves recognizing or making a generalization about a group of specifics.

A main idea lesson consists of three or four short reading selections for which students are asked to identify the main idea.

◆ **Conclusion** Drawing a conclusion is a complex reading skill because a conclusion is not usually stated in a reading passage. Students are asked to draw a conclusion based only on the information within a selection. They must put together the clues as if they were solving a puzzle.

A conclusion lesson contains three or four short reading selections for which students are asked to choose a conclusion that can logically be drawn from the information presented.

◆ **Inference** Students make inferences by combining their own knowledge and experiences with what they read. They must consider all the facts in the reading selection. Then they must put those facts together with what they already know to make a reasonable inference about something that is not stated in the selection. Making an inference, another complex skill, requires students to go beyond the information in the text.

An inference lesson consists of three or four short reading selections. All lessons ask students to choose one logical inference that can be made from the information presented in the selection.

*Biancarosa, G., & Snow, C.E. (2004). *Reading next—A Vision for action and research in middle and high school literacy: A report to Carnegie Corporation of New York*. Washington, D.C.: Alliance for Excellent Education.

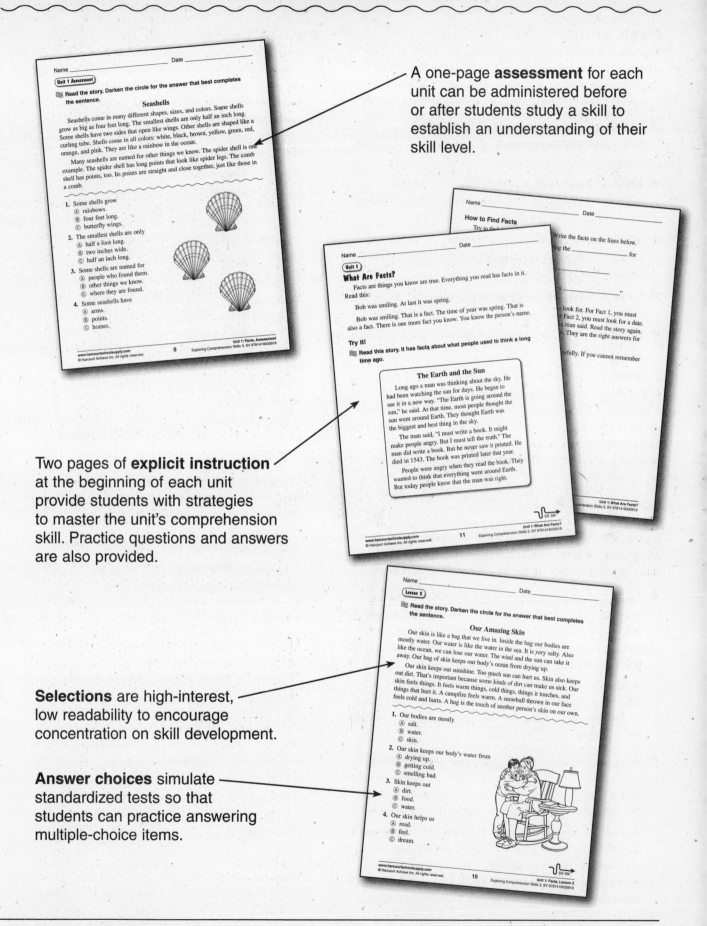

A one-page **assessment** for each unit can be administered before or after students study a skill to establish an understanding of their skill level.

Two pages of **explicit instruction** at the beginning of each unit provide students with strategies to master the unit's comprehension skill. Practice questions and answers are also provided.

Selections are high-interest, low readability to encourage concentration on skill development.

Answer choices simulate standardized tests so that students can practice answering multiple-choice items.

Short-answer questions provide practice for writing on standardized tests.

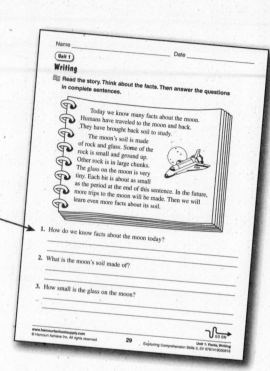

Prewriting graphic organizers guide students to organize ideas for longer writing passages.

On Your Own encourages students to develop their ideas from the graphic organizer into a story.

Name _____ Date _____

≈ **Read the story. Darken the circle for the answer that best completes the sentence.**

Seashells

Seashells come in many different shapes, sizes, and colors. Some shells grow as big as four feet long. The smallest shells are only half an inch long. Some shells have two sides that open like wings. Other shells are shaped like a curling tube. Shells come in all colors: white, black, brown, yellow, green, red, orange, and pink. They are like a rainbow in the ocean.

Many seashells are named for other things we know. The spider shell is one example. The spider shell has long points that look like spider legs. The comb shell has points, too. Its points are straight and close together, just like those in a comb.

1. Some shells grow
   Ⓐ rainbows.
   Ⓑ four feet long.
   Ⓒ butterfly wings.

2. The smallest shells are only
   Ⓐ half a foot long.
   Ⓑ two inches wide.
   Ⓒ half an inch long.

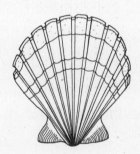

3. Some shells are named for
   Ⓐ people who found them.
   Ⓑ other things we know.
   Ⓒ where they are found.

4. Some seashells have
   Ⓐ arms.
   Ⓑ points.
   Ⓒ homes.

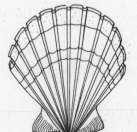

Name _____ Date _____

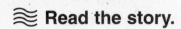

≋ **Read the story.**

Elephants

Elephants are the largest mammals on land. Long ago there were elephants in most countries. Now elephants live only in Africa and Asia. They are smart animals that live together and help each other.

Female elephants live in close family groups. The group is made of mothers and their babies. The young males stay with this group until they are about 14 years old. Then they leave to join a group of male elephants. The males travel in groups, but they are not as close as the family groups. Males often move from one herd to another.

A herd wakes up at four in the morning. The elephants want to start grazing before it gets too hot. They walk to a water hole and drink. The herd walks and eats about 16 hours a day. They eat grass, leaves, bark, and fruit. Sometimes they stop and take naps. At midnight the herd stops for the night. All the elephants lie down and sleep. Some of them snore.

1. Put these events in the order that they happened. What happened first? Write the number **1** on the line by that sentence. Then write the number **2** by the sentence that tells what happened next.

    _____ Elephants live only in Africa and Asia.

    _____ Elephants lived in most countries.

≋ **Darken the circle for the phrase that best answers the question.**

2. When do young males join a male herd?
    Ⓐ when they are about 14
    Ⓑ in the early morning
    Ⓒ when their mothers tell them to

Name _____ Date _____

≋ **Darken the circle for the answer that best completes the sentence.**

Jumping beans _____ because a worm lives inside. The worm lies still when it is cool. But when it gets warm, the worm moves around. Hold a jumping bean in your hand. The heat from your hand will make the worm move. And that makes the bean jump.

1. The word that best completes the sentence is
Ⓐ hear.　　Ⓑ hop.　　Ⓒ push.

Look at the stars. They are different colors. The color tells how hot a star is. The hottest stars are blue. White stars are not quite as hot as blue ones. Then come yellow stars, like our sun. They are even _____ than white stars. The coldest stars are the red ones. But even red stars are too hot to visit.

2. The word that best completes the sentence is
Ⓐ cooler.　　Ⓑ brighter.　　Ⓒ better.

Juliette Gordon Low started the Girl Scouts in America. She had heard about the Boy Scouts. She thought it would be a good idea for girls, too. She believed that girls should learn more than just cooking. They should **explore** the outdoors and take care of themselves while doing so. In 1912 there were 18 Girl Scouts. Now there are 3 million Girl Scouts!

3. In this story, the word **explore** means
Ⓐ walk.　　Ⓑ search.　　Ⓒ paint.

On New Year's Day in China, there is a parade. People dress up and march down the street. A **special** part is the Lion Dance. The lion in the dance is not a real lion. Two people wear a lion suit. One person is the head. The other person is the body. Together they make the lion run, jump, paw the air, and wag its tail.

4. In this story, the word **special** means
Ⓐ important.　　Ⓑ necessary.　　Ⓒ happy.

Unit 4 Assessment

≋ **Darken the circle for the answer that best completes the sentence.**

Lana and her family were getting ready for their summer vacation. They were going to the lake. Lana packed her clothes in a suitcase. Lana also took some books and games. She took her things out to the car. "I'm ready," said Lana. "I can't wait to get to the lake."

1. The story mainly tells
   Ⓐ that Lana was getting ready for a vacation.
   Ⓑ how Lana feels about the lake.
   Ⓒ why Lana wanted to read books and play games.

Baby frogs grow from eggs. How? The mother frog lays her eggs in a pond. The dark center of each egg grows a tail. The eggs have no shells, so the young frog soon starts wiggling around. The baby frog looks like a fish. It swims with its tail and eats tiny water plants. Later it grows four legs and loses its tail. It learns to live both on land and in water.

2. The story mainly tells
   Ⓐ how frogs grow from eggs.
   Ⓑ why eggs have dark centers.
   Ⓒ what eats tiny water plants.

For a long time, sailors have known that sea plants help heal cuts or sores. Now someone has made sea plants into a kind of bandage. It keeps dirt out of skin cuts. It also helps cuts heal.

3. The story mainly tells
   Ⓐ how sea water keeps dirt out of cuts.
   Ⓑ why sailors are always hurting themselves.
   Ⓒ how sea plants are used to heal cuts.

Look at the back of a dollar bill. You will find a circle with an eagle in it. That is the Great Seal of the United States. What do the parts of the seal stand for? The eagle is a strong bird. It stands for might. The bird holds a branch and some arrows. The branch stands for peace. The arrows stand for war. The eagle has a ribbon in its mouth. The writing on the ribbon says, "Out of many states, one nation."

4. The story mainly tells
   Ⓐ what is on the front of a dollar bill.
   Ⓑ what the parts of the Great Seal stand for.
   Ⓒ what the ribbon on the dollar says.

8

Name _____ Date _____

≋ **Darken the circle for the answer that best completes the sentence.**

Many sunken ships lie on the ocean floor. It is hard to raise them. One man found a way. He uses many small balls. Each ball is filled with air so that it floats. He runs a pipe through the inside of the ship. Then he forces the balls through the pipe. Soon the balls fill the ship, and the ship slowly rises.

1. From this story, you can tell
   Ⓐ the man was paid well for his idea.
   Ⓑ the balls are colored blue like the sea.
   Ⓒ the air in each ball helps raise the ship.

Most houses are made of wood, nails, and bricks. But a family in California wanted a house that was different. So they built their house with foam. They laid big sheets of plastic on the ground. Then they used fans to blow air under the sheets. When the sheets looked like large balloons, the family covered the sheets with foam. After the foam dried, they painted it the color of rocks.

2. From this story, you can tell
   Ⓐ the house looked like a rocky hill.
   Ⓑ the house was painted blue and white.
   Ⓒ part of the house was made of bricks.

The first year of life is very important for babies. During this time, they eat their first food. They take their first steps. They say their first words. Babies also grow very fast. They gain about two pounds a month. They also grow ten inches taller. If a child grew this fast every year, a ten-year-old child would be ten feet tall!

3. From this story, you can tell
   Ⓐ older children grow slower than babies.
   Ⓑ people stop learning things after age ten.
   Ⓒ some ten-year-olds are very, very tall.

Name _____ Date _____

≋ **Darken the circle for the sentence that best answers the question.**

One orange is left in the bowl. You touch and smell it. The orange feels soft and mushy. It has a sharp smell. Part of the skin is broken. There is something white and powdery on the skin. You decide not to eat the orange.

1. Which of these sentences is probably true?
   Ⓐ Eating the orange may make you sick.
   Ⓑ The orange is not ripe yet.
   Ⓒ The orange should be used for juice.

The Brooklyn Bridge links Brooklyn and Manhattan in New York. It is very long. The bridge hangs from long steel cables that are sixteen inches thick. Two huge towers hold up the cables. The bridge has six lanes for cars and trucks.

2. Which of these statements is probably true?
   Ⓐ The bridge can hold many cars and trucks.
   Ⓑ The Brooklyn Bridge is a wooden bridge.
   Ⓒ The bridge is never used by people.

American settlers had a hard time moving west. They had to travel over mountains and through thick forests. For years they followed small trails made by Native Americans. In 1811 the government made one of the trails into a road. People could then go all the way from Maryland to Illinois. You can still travel from Washington, D.C., to St. Louis, Missouri, on this road.

3. Which of these sentences is probably true?
   Ⓐ Some roads were once small trails.
   Ⓑ Roads are hard to build.
   Ⓒ Native Americans helped build the road.

Terns are sea birds that are like gulls. A tern is about 15 inches long. It is a strong flier. One kind of tern flies from the North Pole to the South Pole and back each year. Terns eat fish. They build nests near coasts.

4. Which of these sentences is probably true?
   Ⓐ Terns live near the middle of the earth.
   Ⓑ Terns can fly long distances.
   Ⓒ Terns lay three eggs each year.

Unit 1

What Are Facts?

Facts are things you know are true. Everything you read has facts in it. Read this:

Bob was smiling. At last it was spring.

Bob was smiling. That is a fact. The time of year was spring. That is also a fact. There is one more fact you know. You know the person's name.

Try It!

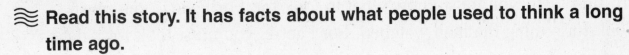 **Read this story. It has facts about what people used to think a long time ago.**

The Earth and the Sun

Long ago a man was thinking about the sky. He had been watching the sun for days. He began to see it in a new way. "The Earth is going around the sun," he said. At that time, most people thought the sun went around Earth. They thought Earth was the biggest and best thing in the sky.

The man said, "I must write a book. It might make people angry. But I must tell the truth." The man did write a book. But he never saw it printed. He died in 1543. The book was printed later that year.

People were angry when they read the book. They wanted to think that everything went around Earth. But today people know that the man was right.

www.harcourtschoolsupply.com
© Harcourt Achieve Inc. All rights reserved.

11

Unit 1: What Are Facts?
Exploring Comprehension Skills 3, SV 9781419030918

How to Find Facts

Try to find the facts in the story. Write the facts on the lines below.

Fact 1: The man had been watching the _____ for days. (moon, Earth, sun)

Fact 2: The man died in the year _____. (1543, 1453, 1457)

Fact 3: The man said, "I must write a _____." (letter, story, book)

• To find facts, you must know what to look for. For Fact 1, you must look for a thing the man watched. For Fact 2, you must look for a date. For Fact 3, you must look for what the man said. Read the story again. Draw a line under *sun*, *1543*, and *book*. They are the right answers for Facts 1, 2, and 3.

• To find the facts, read the story very carefully. If you cannot remember the facts, read the story again.

Name _____   Date _____

≋ **Read the story. Darken the circle for the answer that best completes the sentence.**

Old Glass Bottles

Glass bottles were first made about three thousand years ago. The oldest bottles were made by hand. People blew them into different shapes. Long iron tubes were used to blow the glass. Each person used one tube. People dipped the tubes into melted glass. Then they blew through the tubes. Finally they broke the bottles off the tubes. The tubes left a mark on the finished glass. This mark shows that the glass was blown.

There are other ways to tell if a bottle was made by hand. The glass might have bubbles in it. The bubbles probably came from boiling the glass. Many times the bubbles would stay in the glass as it cooled.

1. Glass bottles were first made
   Ⓐ three thousand years ago.
   Ⓑ four hundred years ago.
   Ⓒ one thousand years ago.

2. People made the oldest bottles
   Ⓐ out of wood.
   Ⓑ with machines.
   Ⓒ by hand.

3. To blow the glass, people used
   Ⓐ glass pots.
   Ⓑ old bottles.
   Ⓒ iron tubes.

4. Bubbles might come from
   Ⓐ soap.
   Ⓑ breaking the glass.
   Ⓒ boiling the glass.

Then people began making glass bottles other ways. They made bottles by pouring the glass into forms. It took two forms to make a bottle. There was one form for each half. Bottles made this way have lines down the sides. That's where the two halves were joined together.

Some old bottles have letters written in the glass. The letters are on the side or the bottom. You can feel them because they stick out. These letters tell the name of the bottle company. There are books that tell about the different companies. The books tell you when and where each bottle was made.

5. People used other ways to
   Ⓐ make bottles.
   Ⓑ blow glass.
   Ⓒ write letters.

6. Bottles with lines down the sides were
   Ⓐ blown with a new kind of tool.
   Ⓑ broken and then fixed.
   Ⓒ poured into two forms.

7. Some bottles have letters on the
   Ⓐ inside of the bottle.
   Ⓑ side or bottom.
   Ⓒ top of the bottle.

8. To find out when a bottle was made,
   Ⓐ use a book that tells about bottle companies.
   Ⓑ learn to blow glass.
   Ⓒ count the lines on the side of the glass.

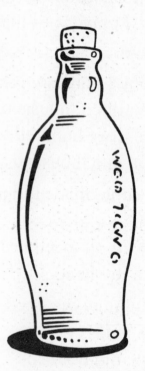

Lesson 2

≋ **Read the story. Darken the circle for the answer that best completes the sentence.**

Our Amazing Skin

Our skin is like a bag that we live in. Inside the bag our bodies are mostly water. Our water is like the water in the sea. It is very salty. Also like the ocean, we can lose our water. The wind and the sun can take it away. Our bag of skin keeps our body's ocean from drying up.

Our skin keeps out sunshine. Too much sun can hurt us. Skin also keeps out dirt. That's important because some kinds of dirt can make us sick. Our skin feels things. It feels warm things, cold things, things it touches, and things that hurt it. A campfire feels warm. A snowball thrown in our face feels cold and hurts. A hug is the touch of another person's skin on our own.

1. Our bodies are mostly
   - Ⓐ salt.
   - Ⓑ water.
   - Ⓒ skin.

2. Our skin keeps our body's water from
   - Ⓐ drying up.
   - Ⓑ getting cold.
   - Ⓒ smelling bad.

3. Skin keeps out
   - Ⓐ dirt.
   - Ⓑ food.
   - Ⓒ water.

4. Our skin helps us
   - Ⓐ read.
   - Ⓑ feel.
   - Ⓒ dream.

Our hair is a special kind of covering. It helps keep things out of our eyes, ears, and nose. Hair is also good for keeping us warm. When we get goose bumps, our body hairs stand up. Then the hairs hold air close to our skin like a thin blanket. Hair keeps animals warm, too. Some animals have more hair than others. So they have a better blanket for cold weather.

Our nails are like very hard skin. They help keep our fingers and toes from getting hurt. Our nails aren't as strong or sharp as the nails that animals have. But they are good for scratching backs and picking up dimes.

5. Hair helps keep things out of our
   Ⓐ fingers and toes.
   Ⓑ mouth and ears.
   Ⓒ eyes, ears, and nose.

6. Hair is good for
   Ⓐ keeping us clean.
   Ⓑ helping us stay warm.
   Ⓒ keeping us from getting hurt.

7. Nails are like
   Ⓐ flat hair.
   Ⓑ hard skin.
   Ⓒ thin blankets.

8. Nails help keep our
   Ⓐ toes sharp.
   Ⓑ fingers from getting loose.
   Ⓒ toes from getting hurt.

Name _____ Date _____

Lesson 3

≋ **Read the story. Darken the circle for the answer that best completes the sentence.**

Snowflake and Little Fish

A tribe of people lived between a beautiful blue lake and a big white mountain. In this tribe lived twin sisters. Their names were Snowflake and Little Fish.

Life was good for the tribe. They had plenty of fish to eat from the lake. They had fresh water from the stream that came down the mountain. The people had everything they needed. But one year things changed. The days grew hot, even in the winter. No snow fell on the mountain. Without melting snow, the stream had no water. And without water from the stream, the lake became dry. Without water in the lake, the fish began to die.

1. Snowflake and Little Fish were twin
   Ⓐ mountains.
   Ⓑ brothers.
   Ⓒ sisters.

2. The people of the tribe
   Ⓐ lived on a white mountain.
   Ⓑ ate chicken in the summer.
   Ⓒ had everything they needed.

3. One year the days were
   Ⓐ wet in the spring.
   Ⓑ cold in the summer.
   Ⓒ hot in the winter.

4. The fish began to
   Ⓐ jump.
   Ⓑ die.
   Ⓒ leave.

GO ON

The women moaned. The men growled. The children cried. The people tried everything they could think of. But nothing worked. One evening Snowflake and Little Fish sat on a rock. They held hands and whispered together for a long time. Their faces were sad, but their eyes were bright. In the morning the sisters were gone. One set of footprints went up the mountain. Another set of footprints went to the lake.

When the sun came up, the mountain was white with snow. Thousands of fish were jumping in the blue lake. The tribe was saved. But no one ever saw Snowflake and Little Fish again.

5. The men
   Ⓐ growled.
   Ⓑ cried.
   Ⓒ moaned.

6. Snowflake and Little Fish
   Ⓐ shouted, "Look at the mountain!"
   Ⓑ danced until the sun came up.
   Ⓒ whispered for a long time.

7. One set of footprints went
   Ⓐ across the grass.
   Ⓑ up the mountain.
   Ⓒ to the fire.

8. When the sun came up, there were
   Ⓐ fish in the lake.
   Ⓑ beautiful stars.
   Ⓒ thousands of birds.

Name _____ Date _____

≋ **Read the story. Darken the circle for the answer that best completes the sentence.**

Working Worms

Many people feel that silk is the finest cloth of all. Just touching silk can be a surprise because it is so soft. Even more surprising is the fact that silk is made by special worms.

If you visited a silk farm, you would see two things: worms and trees. Silkworms eat only the leaves of mulberry trees. So rows and rows of these trees grow on silk farms. On some farms, the leaves are picked by hand. Workers gather leaves from whole branches at once. In other places, machines do this work. The farmers chop the leaves. Then they feed them to their worms.

1. Silk is a type of very fine
   (A) worm.
   (B) tree.
   (C) cloth.

2. At a silk farm, there are worms and
   (A) spiders.
   (B) cows.
   (C) trees.

3. Silkworms eat only
   (A) silk cloth.
   (B) mulberry leaves.
   (C) apple trees.

4. On some farms, the leaves are
   (A) picked by hand.
   (B) cooked in pots.
   (C) left on trees.

↳ **GO ON** →

Name _____   Date _____

Silkworms do nothing but sleep and eat. They grow very quickly. In just four weeks, they become ten thousand times heavier. As the worms grow, they shed their skin four times. The old skin splits and falls off.

The worms are now ready to change into moths. Each worm spins a single long thread of silk around and around itself. This new home is called a cocoon. The thread of each cocoon is as thin as a spider's web. The farmers steam and dry the cocoons. Then the cocoons go to a silk-making plant. There the threads are spun into silk yarn. The yarn will be made into soft cloth that feels like a cloud.

~~~~~~

5. A silkworm grows
   Ⓐ slowly.
   Ⓑ smaller.
   Ⓒ quickly.

6. A silkworm's skin splits and
   Ⓐ gets smaller.
   Ⓑ comes off.
   Ⓒ becomes wet.

7. The thread of each cocoon is
   Ⓐ thin.
   Ⓑ fat.
   Ⓒ red.

8. Silk cloth is very
   Ⓐ rough.
   Ⓑ tight.
   Ⓒ soft.

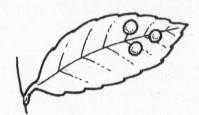

Exploring Comprehension Skills 3, SV 9781419030918

Name _____ Date _____

≈ **Read the story. Darken the circle for the answer that best completes the sentence.**

Hippos

Hippos are animals that live in Africa. Their name means "river horse." But they do not look very much like horses. Hippos have large, round bodies. They have short legs and small ears. They look more like pigs than horses. In fact, hippos and pigs come from the same animal group.

Like pigs, hippos love mud. They stay cool under the hot sun by rolling in mud and swimming in rivers. In spite of their great size, hippos can swim fast. A hippo's eyes and nose stay above the water as it swims. If it dives under the water, it can stay there for as long as five minutes.

1. A hippo's name means
   - Ⓐ mud roller.
   - Ⓑ big diver.
   - Ⓒ river horse.

2. Hippos have
   - Ⓐ no ears.
   - Ⓑ small ears.
   - Ⓒ big ears.

3. Hippos roll in mud to
   - Ⓐ go to sleep.
   - Ⓑ stay cool.
   - Ⓒ get dirty.

4. A hippo can stay underwater for
   - Ⓐ five minutes.
   - Ⓑ one day.
   - Ⓒ five hours.

Baby hippos can run and swim when they are born. They can get milk from their mothers underwater. Baby hippos stay with their mothers for years. When they go for a walk, the babies line up behind their mothers. The mothers lead them along like ducks.

Baby hippos love to play. They dive in the river and blow water from their noses. Sometimes they swim on top of their parents' backs or heads. But they cannot do this when they are grown. Grown hippos weigh as much as four tons.

5. Baby hippos can
   Ⓐ fly.
   Ⓑ talk.
   Ⓒ swim.

6. Baby hippos stay with their mothers for
   Ⓐ months.
   Ⓑ years.
   Ⓒ weeks.

7. Hippos are like ducks when they
   Ⓐ start swimming.
   Ⓑ are sleeping.
   Ⓒ go for a walk.

8. Grown hippos can weigh up to
   Ⓐ four pounds.
   Ⓑ four tons.
   Ⓒ ten tons.

Name _____ Date _____

Lesson 6

≋ **Read the story. Darken the circle for the answer that best completes the sentence.**

The Name Game

Years ago people had only one name. Each name had a special meaning. A baby might be given a name that meant "brave" or "bright." The parents hoped that the child would live up to the name. They thought that a good name would help the child.

Then towns got larger. Sometimes people with the same name lived close to one another. Their friends had to have a way to tell them apart. So people began to have longer names. The new names told something about the person.

1. Years ago people had only one
   Ⓐ hat.
   Ⓑ baby.
   Ⓒ name.

2. Each name had
   Ⓐ a special meaning.
   Ⓑ the same letters.
   Ⓒ one correct spelling.

3. Sometimes people had
   Ⓐ too many names.
   Ⓑ the same name.
   Ⓒ two towns.

4. The new names told about the
   Ⓐ parents.
   Ⓑ town.
   Ⓒ person.

Unit 1: Facts, Lesson 6
Exploring Comprehension Skills 3, SV 9781419030918

Sometimes the names told where a person lived. If there were two Johns, one might have been called John of the Woods. Maybe the other John had red hair. He would have been called John the Red.

By about the year 1300, most people had two names. They also started to give their names to their children. Many of these last names are still used today. Lincoln was a town in England. *Johnson* meant "son of John." Smiths were workers who used hammers. They worked with metal, wood, or stone.

5. John the Red had
   Ⓐ red hair.
   Ⓑ brown eyes.
   Ⓒ black teeth.

6. By about 1300, people gave their children
   Ⓐ their own rooms.
   Ⓑ more money.
   Ⓒ two names.

7. Lincoln was a
   Ⓐ road.
   Ⓑ town.
   Ⓒ mountain.

8. Smiths worked with
   Ⓐ saws.
   Ⓑ hammers.
   Ⓒ knives.

Name _____ Date _____

≋ **Read the story. Darken the circle for the answer that best completes the sentence.**

A Cowboy's Life

Did you ever see an old TV show or movie about cowboys? It made their life seem fun and exciting all the time. But a real cowboy's life was mainly hard work. Most cowboys worked on a ranch. They had to keep an eye on cows in the herd. Sometimes cows tried to run away. Cowboys had to chase them down and bring them back.

Many cows were sold to buyers far away. So cowboys went on trail drives. They led the cows to the buyers in other towns. The trail could be one thousand miles or more. A trail drive could last two or three months.

1. A TV show makes a cowboy's life seem
   Ⓐ hard.
   Ⓑ fun.
   Ⓒ long.

2. Most real cowboys worked on a
   Ⓐ ranch.
   Ⓑ farm.
   Ⓒ home.

3. A cowboy kept an eye mostly on
   Ⓐ fires.
   Ⓑ horses.
   Ⓒ cows.

4. A trail drive could last
   Ⓐ two years.
   Ⓑ two or three months.
   Ⓒ one day.

Cowboys needed good, strong horses. They rode them all day long. Sometimes they rode part of the night, too. The horses were called "cow ponies." They had to be fast and smart. They had to sense a cow's every move. The horses worked as hard as their riders did!

Cowboys also wore special clothing. Their hats had wide brims. This kept sun and rain off their faces. They also used hats to scoop water from a stream. Cowboys wore vests instead of coats. These vests had pockets to hold coins or a watch. Cowboys also wore tall, rugged boots for long rides.

5. Cowboys rode their horses
   Ⓐ all day.
   Ⓑ once a week.
   Ⓒ every other day.

6. A horse had to sense
   Ⓐ when other horses were near.
   Ⓑ when a rider was tired.
   Ⓒ what a cow might do next.

7. A cowboy hat had a wide brim to
   Ⓐ put coins in.
   Ⓑ keep the hat on tighter.
   Ⓒ protect the cowboy's face.

8. While riding, cowboys wore
   Ⓐ sneakers.
   Ⓑ moccasins.
   Ⓒ boots.

Lesson 8

≋ **Read the story. Darken the circle for the answer that best completes the sentence.**

An Amazing Life

Helen Keller became ill while she was still a baby. The illness caused her to lose her sight and hearing. Because she could not see or hear, she did not know how to speak. Helen was shut off from the rest of the world.

At age 7, Helen was given a private teacher. Her name was Anne Sullivan. Anne was nearly blind as a child. She knew how it felt not to see. Anne taught Helen through touch. She spelled out letters on Helen's hand. The letters spelled the names of things. Anne placed those things in Helen's hand. Soon Helen knew how to spell words.

1. Helen's illness caused her to
   Ⓐ lose her taste.
   Ⓑ lose her touch.
   Ⓒ lose her sight and hearing.

2. As a child, Helen
   Ⓐ could only whisper.
   Ⓑ spoke normally.
   Ⓒ was not able to speak.

3. Anne Sullivan taught Helen
   Ⓐ by phone.
   Ⓑ through music.
   Ⓒ through touch.

4. Anne spelled letters on Helen's
   Ⓐ throat.
   Ⓑ hand.
   Ⓒ eyes.

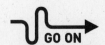

Helen wanted to learn more. At age 10, she began to learn to speak. Her teacher spoke to her. Helen placed a finger on the speaker's lips and throat. By age 16, Helen could speak pretty well. She went to college and made top grades.

After college Helen worked to help other people who were blind. She taught them to have hope and to be brave. She wrote many books about her life. She gave speeches all over the world. She raised lots of money for those who were blind. Helen Keller became a hero to people everywhere.

5. At age 10, Helen started to learn
   Ⓐ to talk.
   Ⓑ to sing.
   Ⓒ to write.

6. Helen felt a speaker's
   Ⓐ nose and ears.
   Ⓑ eyes and hands.
   Ⓒ throat and lips.

7. Helen wrote books about
   Ⓐ famous people.
   Ⓑ her own life.
   Ⓒ how the brain works.

8. Helen helped people who were blind by
   Ⓐ raising money for them.
   Ⓑ letting Anne teach them.
   Ⓒ becoming a doctor.

Name _____ Date _____

Writing

≋ **Read the story. Think about the facts. Then answer the questions in complete sentences.**

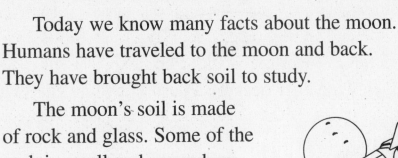

Today we know many facts about the moon. Humans have traveled to the moon and back. They have brought back soil to study.

The moon's soil is made of rock and glass. Some of the rock is small and ground up. Other rock is in large chunks. The glass on the moon is very tiny. Each bit is about as small as the period at the end of this sentence. In the future, more trips to the moon will be made. Then we will learn even more facts about its soil.

1. How do we know facts about the moon today?

_____

_____

2. What is the moon's soil made of?

_____

_____

3. How small is the glass on the moon?

_____

_____

29

Unit 1: Facts, Writing
Exploring Comprehension Skills 3, SV 9781419030918

Prewriting

≋ Think of an idea you might write about, such as a place you visited or an item you found. Write the idea in the center of the idea web below. Then fill out the rest of the web with facts.

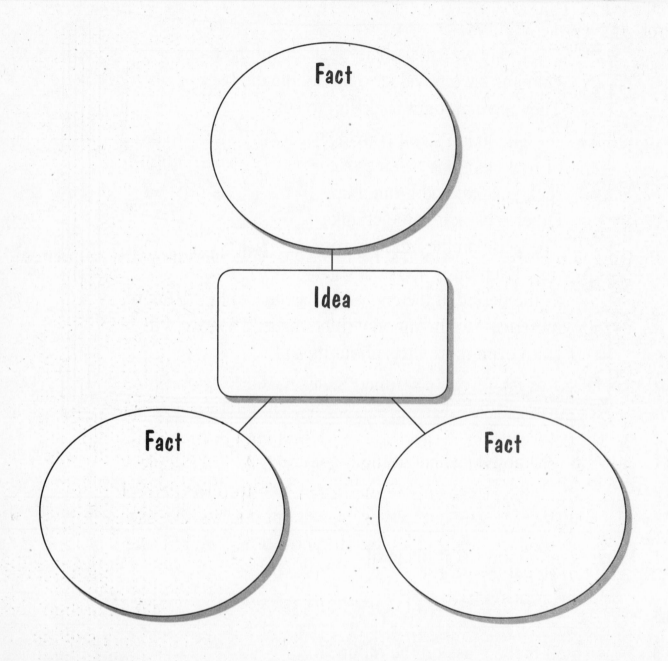

On Your Own

≋ Now use another sheet of paper to write a story about your idea. Use the facts from the idea web.

Unit 2

What Is Sequence?

Sequence means *time order*. When things happen in a story, they happen in a sequence. Something happens first. Then other things happen. Then something happens last. How can you find the sequence in a story? Just look for clue words, like these:

today	then	Monday
first	after	June

Try It!

≋ **Here is a story about apples. See whether you can follow the sequence. Circle all the clue words.**

Apples

People in the United States have liked apples for many years. But apple trees have not always grown in this part of the world. People brought the trees with them about four hundred years ago. At first people planted trees only in the East. Later, travelers carried them west. Now apples grow in most states. We use them in pies and jellies. But most of all, we just like to eat them raw.

www.harcourtschoolsupply.com
© Harcourt Achieve Inc. All rights reserved.

31

Unit 2: What Is Sequence?
Exploring Comprehension Skills 3, SV 9781419030918

How to Find Sequence

Try to follow the sequence in the story about apples. On this page, there are two sentences about the story. Write the number **1** on the line by the sentence that tells what happened first. Write the number **2** by the sentence that tells what happened next.

_____ Travelers carried apple trees west.

_____ People planted apple trees in the East.

• Read all the words in the two sentences above. Now read the story about apples again. Try to find the words in the two sentences that are in the story. Did you find the words *travelers* and *East* in the story? Draw a line under these two words.

• After you find the words *travelers* and *East*, find the clue words that are close by. The clue words that go with East are *at first*. The clue word that goes with *travelers* is *later*. The clue words tell you how to put things in a sequence. *At first* tells you that something happened at the very beginning. *Later* tells you that something happened after something else.

• If you still cannot find the sequence, try this. Look at the sentences in the story. One sentence is first. Another sentence is second, and another one is third. The sentences are in order. The action in the first sentence happened first, and the action in the second sentence happened second.

The correct sequence of the sentences is 2, 1.

www.harcourtschoolsupply.com
© Harcourt Achieve Inc. All rights reserved.

32

Unit 2: What Is Sequence?
Exploring Comprehension Skills 3, SV 9781419030918

Lesson 1

≋ **Read the story.**

The Dai Family, Americans

The Dai family had been living in America for five years. One night Mrs. Dai said, "We must talk about something. We left Vietnam in fear. We had to run and hide. At last we came to America. No one tries to hurt us here. Now we have the chance to be Americans. But if we become Americans, we will no longer be Vietnamese. What should we do?" The Dais talked for a long time.

Then Mr. Dai said, "I'm proud that I was born in Vietnam. But the country we loved is not there anymore. We can't go back. It would be good if we became Americans."

One bright Saturday Mr. Dai went to the library and got some books. He asked the children for help. They had been going to school. They helped their parents learn to read English. The Dais read about how Americans choose their president.

Then the Dais took some tests. Next the Dais filled out some papers. People checked the papers. They also checked to make sure the Dais had not broken any laws. After a month, the family got a letter from a judge. He wanted to see them on Monday. On that day, they put on their best clothes and went to the judge. First the judge asked Mr. and Mrs. Dai if they would follow the laws. They both said they would. Next the judge had them raise their right hands. They said they would be true to America. The judge said, "You are now Americans."

1. Put these events in the order that they happened. What happened first?
Write the number **1** on the line by that sentence. Then write the number **2**
by the sentence that tells what happened next.

_____ The Dais took some tests.

_____ The Dais filled out papers.

≋ **Darken the circle for the phrase that best answers the question.**

2. When did Mr. and Mrs. Dai learn to read English?
   Ⓐ while they lived in Vietnam
   Ⓑ after the judge said they were Americans
   Ⓒ before they went to see the judge

3. When did the judge see the Dais?
   Ⓐ on Monday
   Ⓑ on Wednesday
   Ⓒ one bright Saturday

4. What did the judge ask the Dais first?
   Ⓐ if they would raise their right hands
   Ⓑ if they promised to follow the laws
   Ⓒ if they promised to be true to America

Lesson 2

≋ **Read the story.**

Sky-Father-in-Heaven

Some Native Americans tell this story. It is about how they think the world began.

Long, long ago, Sky-Father-in-Heaven was alone. He had no one to be his friend. So he decided to make some new things.

Sky-Father rolled a piece of dark night into a ball. He looked at the ball with his big eyes. It began to shine with a bright light. "This will be the sun," Sky-Father said. He put the sun high in the sky. He then made little balls of night. He looked at the balls, and they also began to shine. He made these the stars.

 Next Sky-Father took another ball of night. He held it close to his heart. This ball of night became the earth. Then Sky-Father cried. His tears filled up all the seas. He put the earth near the sun. Grass and trees grew on the earth.

But Sky-Father was still lonely. He took yellow clay from the earth. He made a yellow man. Then he made a black man from black earth. He mixed sand with water and made a white man. Next he took more dirt and made a red man and a brown man. He baked the five men in an oven. When he took them out, they were not made of dirt anymore. He put his hands on the men, and they came to life. At last Sky-Father took wind, water, and dirt. He made First Woman from these. Then Sky-Father put the five men and First Woman on the earth. He wasn't lonely anymore.

1. Put these events in the order that they happened. What happened first?
Write the number **1** on the line by that sentence. Then write the number **2**
by the sentence that tells what happened next.

_____ Sky-Father's tears filled the seas.

_____ Sky-Father held a ball of night to his heart.

≋ **Darken the circle for the phrase that best answers the question.**

2. When did Sky-Father make the stars?
Ⓐ before he made the men
Ⓑ before he made the sun
Ⓒ after he made the earth

3. When did Sky-Father make the earth?
Ⓐ after he made First Woman
Ⓑ after he made the men
Ⓒ after he made the sun and stars

4. When did Sky-Father make a brown man?
Ⓐ before he made a yellow man
Ⓑ after he made First Woman
Ⓒ after he made a black man

Lesson 3

≋ **Read the story.**

A Cowboy's Day

It was a cool spring morning. The cook shouted, "Everyone up! Get your food before I throw it out!" The sleeping cowboys woke up and stretched. They went to the cook's wagon for breakfast.

All winter the cattle had been out in the fields. They ran wild and ate grass. But now the owners wanted to see how many cattle they had. So the cowboys had to find the cattle and catch them. They called this "rounding up the cattle."

After breakfast the men got on their best horses and rode away. Soon they found some cattle in a field. The cowboys rode around the herd. Then they started moving the cattle. The animals were afraid, and some didn't want to go. But the cowboys kept them moving. Finally they got to a big, wooden pen.

Then the cowboys looked at the cattle. Some of the cattle had a mark burned into their hair. The marks showed who owned the cattle. But the young cows didn't have any marks. They had been born just that winter. When a cowboy saw a calf without a mark, he caught it with a rope. He knew who owned the calf because each mother cow had a mark. The calf had to be given the same mark the mother cow had. The cowboys pressed a hot iron into the calf's fur.

Soon all the calves were marked. Late that night, the cowboys would have a little party. They would joke, sing, and tell stories.

Name _____ Date _____

1. Put these events in the order that they happened. What happened first?
   Write the number **1** on the line by that sentence. Then write the number **2**
   by the sentence that tells what happened next.

   _____ The men caught calves with a rope.

   _____ The cowboys looked at the cattle.

≋ **Darken the circle for the phrase that best answers the question.**

2. When were the cattle brought to the pen?
   Ⓐ after the cowboys found the cattle
   Ⓑ when the cook shouted
   Ⓒ after the cowboys had a party

3. When did the cowboys put marks on the cattle?
   Ⓐ before they ate breakfast in the morning
   Ⓑ when they first found them in the field
   Ⓒ when the cattle got to the big pen

4. When did the cowboys have a party?
   Ⓐ before all the calves had been marked
   Ⓑ late at night
   Ⓒ when they ate breakfast

Lesson 4

≈ **Read the story.**

Coming to America

"Anton sent a letter from America!" Mrs. Novak cried. "Stan, will you read it to us?" Stan read the letter. It said: "I have found work that pays well. I have meat three times a week. But I miss you. Here is money to pay for Stan to come over. He and I will work hard and save our money. Then you, my dear parents, can come. With great love and hope, Anton."

The next day Mrs. Novak put Stan's clothes in a bag. She put bread, cheese, and dry meat in a basket. Mr. Novak said, "Go with our blessing. Love your new land. But do not forget Poland." Then Stan walked the thirty miles to the sea.

At last Stan got on a big boat. He did not have much money, so he stayed in a large room with many people. People slept on shelves. There were no beds. It was very crowded, and it smelled bad. Sometimes high waves made the boat rock. Sometimes Stan got sick from the rocking. The trip lasted six long weeks. One cloudy day someone shouted, "Land! We are here at last!" Stan ran to look. Some people were so happy they cried.

The boat came to an island. Then people got off and stood in long lines. Doctors looked at them to see if they were healthy. Other people asked many questions. They asked, "Have you broken laws? Can you work?" At last Stan was sent to a small boat that took him off the island and to the mainland. Then Stan began the walk to Anton's home and to his new life.

GO ON

Exploring Comprehension Skills 3, SV 9781419030918

1. Put these events in the order that they happened. What happened first? Write the number **1** on the line by that sentence. Then write the number **2** by the sentence that tells what happened next.

_____ Stan Novak got on the boat in Poland.

_____ Anton Novak wrote to his family in Poland.

≋ **Darken the circle for the phrase that best answers the question.**

2. When did Stan Novak walk thirty miles?
   Ⓐ after he got to America
   Ⓑ after he got sick on the boat
   Ⓒ before he got to the big boat

3. When did people ask Stan many questions?
   Ⓐ before his family got the letter
   Ⓑ before he got on the big boat
   Ⓒ after he landed on the island

4. When did Stan walk to Anton's home?
   Ⓐ before people asked him many questions
   Ⓑ after a small boat took him off of the island
   Ⓒ during the long boat trip on the sea

Lesson 5

≋ **Read the story.**

The Brothers Grimm

You know who Snow White is. You've heard of Hansel and Gretel. But have you heard of the Brothers Grimm? If not for them, you might never have heard these tales.

Jakob and Wilhelm Grimm were the oldest of six children. Jakob was born in 1785. Wilhelm was born the next year. They were the best of friends. The brothers lived and worked together for most of their lives.

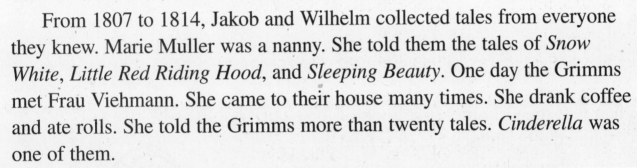

In 1798 the Grimms moved to the town of Cassel. There they finished school. Then they found jobs in the king's library. Both men loved old stories. In their free time, they searched for old folktales and songs.

From 1807 to 1814, Jakob and Wilhelm collected tales from everyone they knew. Marie Muller was a nanny. She told them the tales of *Snow White*, *Little Red Riding Hood*, and *Sleeping Beauty*. One day the Grimms met Frau Viehmann. She came to their house many times. She drank coffee and ate rolls. She told the Grimms more than twenty tales. *Cinderella* was one of them.

In 1812 the Grimms' first book of fairy tales was published. The Grimms had meant the stories for grown-ups. They were surprised when children loved them, too. They wanted to find more tales. This time it was much easier. Now people would bring stories to them. The next book of tales was published in 1815. The last book of *Grimm's Fairy Tales* was published in 1857.

GO ON

Name _____ Date _____

1. Put these events in the order that they happened. What happened first?
Write the number **1** on the line by that sentence. Then write the number **2**
by the sentence that tells what happened next.

_____ The brothers finished school.

_____ The brothers collected tales.

≋ **Darken the circle for the phrase that best answers the question.**

2. When was Wilhelm Grimm born?
   Ⓐ the year before Jakob was born
   Ⓑ in 1785
   Ⓒ the year after Jakob was born

3. When did the brothers collect tales from friends?
   Ⓐ from 1807 to 1814
   Ⓑ in 1798
   Ⓒ when they were children

4. When was the Grimms' first book of fairy tales published?
   Ⓐ when the brothers were in school
   Ⓑ after they began working in the library
   Ⓒ from 1807 to 1814

Exploring Comprehension Skills 3, SV 9781419030918

Lesson 6

≈ **Read the story.**

The Great White Bear

In some languages, they are called snow bears or ice bears. We call them polar bears. These giants live in the arctic lands of the far north. Only a few creatures are strong enough to live in such a cold, empty place. Polar bears live alone except when a mother bear has cubs. Female bears have cubs every three years. Like most bears, they are good mothers.

Polar bears mate in April. In September the female goes back to the place she was born. She looks for a den. In December the mother gives birth to two cubs. The cubs are smaller than human babies, and they are just as helpless.

By March the cubs weigh 25 pounds. It is time for them to see the world. They leave the den. At first they are cold and puzzled. They slip and slide as they try to walk on the ice.

Later in the spring, the mother leads the cubs to the seashore. They must catch seals before the ice melts and the seals leave. The cubs walk in their mother's tracks. She teaches them to sniff the air for food. Polar bears can smell food as far as ten miles away.

When they arrive at the seashore, she teaches them how to catch seals. She shows them how to swim in the icy water. When they are two years old, the cubs leave their mother. She has taught them everything they need to know to live on their own.

1. Put these events in the order that they happened. What happened first?
   Write the number **1** on the line by that sentence. Then write the number **2**
   by the sentence that tells what happened next.

   _____ The mother and cubs stay in the den until March.

   _____ The female bear returns to the place she
   was born.

≋ **Darken the circle for the phrase that best answers the question.**

2. When do polar bears mate?
   Ⓐ in April
   Ⓑ when they are two years old
   Ⓒ in September

3. When are the cubs born?
   Ⓐ later in the spring
   Ⓑ in December
   Ⓒ when the mother arrives at the seashore

4. When do the cubs leave their mother?
   Ⓐ when they come out of the den
   Ⓑ when they are three months old
   Ⓒ after they learn to catch seals

Lesson 7

≈ **Read the story.**

A Secret King

A king wanted to see what his people were really like. So he put on rags and went for a walk. After a while, he got tired and hungry. But when he asked people for food, they laughed and threw rocks at him. They did not know who the poor man was.

Then the king came to an old house. A poor old man and woman lived there. They asked the king to eat with them. They didn't know he was the king. They just wanted to help a tired, hungry man. The woman made a fire. Then she brought cool water for the king to drink. While she was doing this, the old man went outside. He picked some food from the tiny garden. Then he tried to catch a chicken for supper. But the chicken ran fast, and the old man was tired. So he chose some eggs instead.

The woman cooked supper for them. When the food was ready, she put it on the table. The king was given the best food. Suddenly there was a knock at the door. The old woman opened it and saw some neighbors.

"Great King, forgive us," they said. "We threw rocks because we did not recognize you."

The king was angry. "I was tired and hungry. You gave me only rocks and bad words. Get out of here!" he shouted.

The poor man and woman were afraid. The king was used to nice food, but they had given him only bread and eggs. The king said, "You gave me the best you had. Because you were kind, I will give money and food to you for the rest of your lives."

1. Put these events in the order that they happened. What happened first?
Write the number **1** on the line by that sentence. Then write the number **2**
by the sentence that tells what happened next.

_____ The man and woman asked the king to dinner.

_____ The king put on rags and went for a walk.

≈ **Darken the circle for the phrase that best answers the question.**

2. When did the people of the town throw rocks?
   Ⓐ after the king stopped at the old house
   Ⓑ when the king asked them for food
   Ⓒ when the king shouted "Get out of here!"

3. When did the old man get the food for supper?
   Ⓐ while the old woman made fire
   Ⓑ before the people threw rocks
   Ⓒ after the neighbors knocked on the door

4. When did the woman give the king water?
   Ⓐ before he dressed in rags and went walking
   Ⓑ after the neighbors came by the house
   Ⓒ after she made a fire to cook supper

≋ **Read the story.**

Mule Deer

Mule deer are a type of deer that live in western North America. They are known for the strange way they run. They push off the ground with all four feet at once, much like a jackrabbit. Some mule deer live in thick woods on mountains. Others live in dry, empty deserts. Some live near the West Coast. Although they can live in many places, mule deer don't like to live near people.

Mule deer are beautiful animals. They are named for their big, soft mule-like ears. In the summer, the deer are reddish-brown. In the winter, they are grayish-brown. They change their coats in the spring and fall. In this way, they blend in with the colors of the trees and grass around them.

The male mule deer, or bucks, grow antlers each year. The antlers begin to grow in April or May. At first they are soft and velvety. They grow through the summer and stop in September. Then the velvet is shed. There is hard bone beneath. In February, the antlers fall off. Most antlers have four points. They can grow to be more than two feet long.

A mule deer eats early in the morning and just before the sun sets. The deer must eat quickly. When it is out in the open, it is in danger from enemies. It chews the grass only enough for it to be swallowed. Then it goes to a more sheltered place. There it can relax.

GO ON

1. Put these events in the order that they happened. What happened first? Write the number **1** on the line by that sentence. Then write the number **2** by the sentence that tells what happened next.

_____ In February, the antlers fall off.

_____ The antlers are soft and velvety.

≈ **Darken the circle for the phrase that best answers the question.**

2. When is the deer's coat reddish brown?
- Ⓐ when the deer is one year old
- Ⓑ in the spring and the fall
- Ⓒ during the summer

3. How often do bucks grow antlers?
- Ⓐ each year
- Ⓑ every two years
- Ⓒ only once

4. When is the velvet shed from the antlers?
- Ⓐ when the antlers begin to grow
- Ⓑ during the spring
- Ⓒ after the antlers stop growing

Name _____ Date _____

Writing

≋ **Read the story. Think about the sequence, or time order. Then answer the questions in complete sentences.**

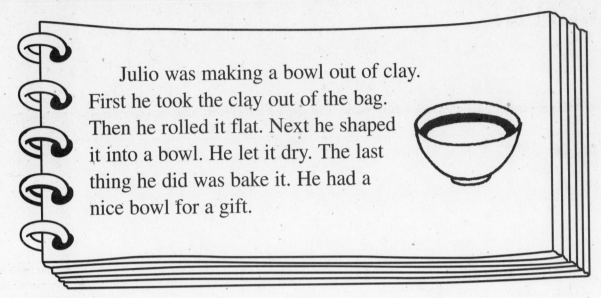

Julio was making a bowl out of clay. First he took the clay out of the bag. Then he rolled it flat. Next he shaped it into a bowl. He let it dry. The last thing he did was bake it. He had a nice bowl for a gift.

1. What did Julio do first?

_____

_____

2. What did Julio do after he made the clay flat?

_____

_____

3. What did Julio do before he baked the bowl?

_____

_____

GO ON

Name _____ Date _____

Prewriting

 Think about something that you have done, such as planting a garden, catching a fish, or washing a dog. Write the events in sequence below.

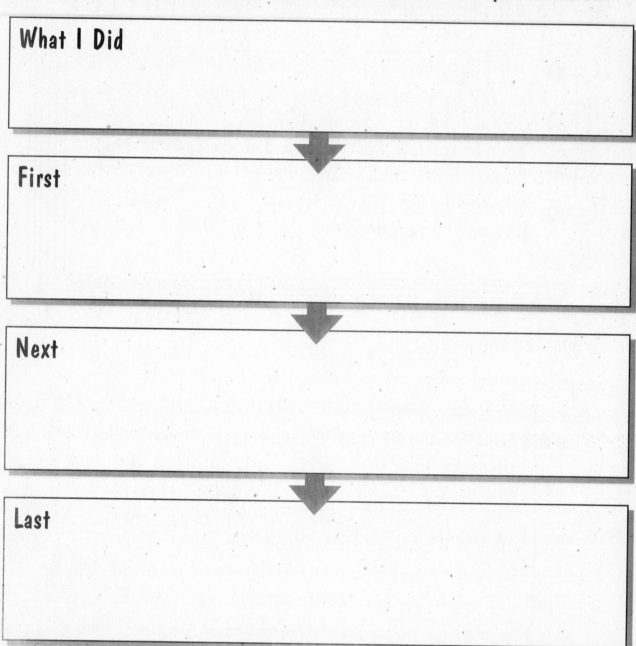

What I Did

First

Next

Last

On Your Own

 Now use another sheet of paper to write a story about what you have done. Write the events in the order that they happened. Use time order words.

Unit 3

What Is Context?

You can use context to learn new words. If you find a word you do not know, look at the words around it. These other words can help you guess what the word means.

Look at the words below. Choose a word and write it on the line.

Bats hunt at night and sleep during the _____.

Did you write *day*? Why did you write that word? Some words go together. *Day* goes with *night*. The context helped you choose the right word.

Try It!

≈ **Read the story below. It has a word you may not know. The word is printed in *dark letters*. See if you can find out what the new word means.**

Chuck Berry Makes a Hit

The singer named Muddy Waters listened to the young man. He really liked to hear him sing. He **encouraged** Chuck to make a record. "You're really good!" he said. "Go ahead and try to make the big time." Chuck's first record had a new kind of music. It was called rock and roll. Today many people say that Chuck Berry is the father of rock and roll.

www.harcourtschoolsupply.com
© Harcourt Achieve Inc. All rights reserved.

51

Unit 3: What Is Context?
Exploring Comprehension Skills 3, SV 9781419030918

How to Use Context

If you don't know what **encouraged** means, look at the context. Remember, the context is all the other words in the story. Here are some of the other words in the story. They can help you find out what **encouraged** means.

1. "You're really good!"

2. "Go ahead and try to make the big time."

Find these words in the story about Chuck Berry. Draw a circle around them. What words do you think of when you read the clues? Write a few words on the lines below:

_____

_____

Did you write a word like *help*? To **encourage** someone is to help someone by what you say or do.

• To use context, read all the words in a story. If some words are too hard, don't stop! Read all the words you can. They may tell you something about the words you could not read.

• When you try to find out what new words mean, remember that some words go together. Think of a meaning that goes with the other words in the story.

www.harcourtschoolsupply.com
© Harcourt Achieve Inc. All rights reserved.

52

Unit 3: What Is Context?
Exploring Comprehension Skills 3, SV 9781419030918

Lesson 1

≈ **Darken the circle for the answer that best completes the sentence.**

When Philip was a boy, settlers came to live near his tribe. Philip's father was chief then. He and the settlers made a peace _____. Later, Philip became chief. He was called King Philip. He was upset with the settlers. They had built their homes on the tribe's land. King Philip started a war with the settlers. He was killed in the war. The tribe lost its land forever.

1. The word that best completes the sentence is
   Ⓐ sand.　　Ⓑ color.　　Ⓒ treaty.

Marbles are made at a factory. Workers first make glass in a large tank. They heat the tank to make the glass hot. Hot glass is thick like syrup. It is poured from a hole at the bottom of the tank. The glass is cut into small chunks. These bits of glass are put on rollers. The rollers change the glass into smooth round balls. They become marbles. The marbles are sorted by size and color. Then they are put into large _____.

2. The word that best completes the sentence is
   Ⓐ bins.　　Ⓑ friends.　　Ⓒ stars.

An underground cave can have a stream in it. A cave fish lives in this stream. The fish is small and white. It can't see because it doesn't have any _____. It doesn't need them since there is no light in the cave. The cave fish finds food by smell and feel.

3. The word that best completes the sentence is
   Ⓐ arms.　　Ⓑ eyes.　　Ⓒ teeth.

Mangrove trees grow in salt water. Most trees take in water with their roots. Then they let it out through their leaves. When mangroves take in water, they take in salt, too. They let the water and the salt out. After that, mangroves look as if someone _____ salt all over their leaves.

4. The word that best completes the sentence is
   Ⓐ threw.　　Ⓑ liked.　　Ⓒ grew.

Lesson 2

≋ **Darken the circle for the answer that best completes the sentence.**

Death Valley is in California. There is a very old, dry lake bed there. It is called the Racetrack. Marks on the ground show that large rocks there have moved. Some people think that the rocks move because of the weather. When it rains there, the dirt gets muddy. Then strong winds blow the rocks over the _____ ground. The rocks leave marks in the mud. After the mud dries, the marks can still be seen.

1. The word that best completes the sentence is
Ⓐ beautiful. Ⓑ foolish. Ⓒ slippery.

Gerbils are small, furry creatures. They have long back legs and a long, hairy tail. Gerbils are _____ and love to play. They are easy to care for and fun to watch. That is why gerbils make such good pets.

2. The word that best completes the sentence is
Ⓐ frisky. Ⓑ lazy. Ⓒ sleepy.

People have taken over much of the land. Many wild creatures have lost their homes. Some people worry about this. A few of them formed a group. The group is called the World Wildlife Fund. This group works to save animals and their homes. Many animals live in the rain _____. The World Wildlife Fund works to keep the trees there from being cut down.

3. The word that best completes the sentence is
Ⓐ drops. Ⓑ beds. Ⓒ forests.

Juan Largo has spent seven years learning about black bears. He catches the bears. Then he puts little radios on them. He can track the bears and _____ down what they do. He even knows where they sleep during the winter. Sometimes he puts a tag on a bear's ear. Then he will know that bear when he sees it again.

4. The word that best completes the sentence is
Ⓐ back. Ⓑ write. Ⓒ sing.

Name _____ Date _____

≈ **Darken the circle for the answer that best completes the sentence.**

There are different ways to show what the world looks like. One way is a map. A map is a flat drawing of the world. Another way to show the world is a _____. This shows that the world is round.

1. The word that best completes the sentence is
   Ⓐ sandwich.   Ⓑ flash.   Ⓒ globe.

People who work with metal are called welders. They join pieces of metal together. Welders use _____ to make the metal hot. They melt the edges of the pieces and join them together. When the pieces cool, they stay together. Welders always have to think about safety when they work. They wear special clothes so they won't be hurt.

2. The word that best completes the sentence is
   Ⓐ flashlights.   Ⓑ torches.   Ⓒ scissors.

A parrot is a bird that can talk. It copies the sounds it hears. This bird has special _____ in its neck. The parrot tightens and loosens them. That's how it makes the sounds it hears. A wild parrot sounds like other parrots. But a pet parrot can bark like a dog, ring like a phone, or talk like a person. A pet parrot can even sing and whistle.

3. The word that best completes the sentence is
   Ⓐ candy.   Ⓑ bottles.   Ⓒ muscles.

A young girl was taken from her home and made a slave. She was brought to the United States and sold. The Wheatley family bought her. Her name was changed to Phillis Wheatley. Her new family taught her how to read and write. Phillis started writing poems. Later she was freed. She once sent a poem to George Washington. He _____ her poem very much. He asked Phillis to visit him.

4. The word that best completes the sentence is
   Ⓐ admired.   Ⓑ wore.   Ⓒ rode.

Name _____ Date _____

≋ **Darken the circle for the answer that best completes the sentence.**

A beaver's house is called a lodge. The lodge is built on a pond or a river. It is made with branches and twigs. The beaver enters the lodge from a tunnel under the water. Inside the lodge is a room. The _____ of the room is above the water. The beaver can dry off and stay warm in the room of its lodge.

1. The word that best completes the sentence is
   Ⓐ floor.   Ⓑ knee.   Ⓒ shoe.

Charles Drew was good in sports. He wanted to teach others how to play sports. So he became a _____ . Later, Charles went back to school. He wanted to be a doctor. While in school, Charles studied about blood. He found a way to store blood. Then it could be used when it was needed. Many people's lives were saved. Charles won many awards for his work.

2. The word that best completes the sentence is
   Ⓐ pilot.   Ⓑ dancer.   Ⓒ coach.

Mount St. Helens is a volcano. It is in the state of Washington. It was quiet for almost fifty years. Then one day Mount St. Helens exploded. Ash was thrown into the air. Lava flowed, and hot rocks flew out. Melting snow caused floods. Forests caught on fire. The _____ where people stayed were burned. Some people lost their lives.

3. The word that best completes the sentence is
   Ⓐ cabins.   Ⓑ meals.   Ⓒ nights.

A shooting star looks like a streak of light in the sky. It's a piece of metal or stone called a meteor. It passes through the air around Earth. It gets very hot. It gets so hot that it glows. Sometimes there are many in the sky at once. It looks as if it's raining shooting stars. This is called a meteor _____ .

4. The word that best completes the sentence is
   Ⓐ television.   Ⓑ shower.   Ⓒ zoo.

Lesson 5

≋ **Darken the circle for the answer that best completes the sentence.**

A rodeo is great fun. It reminds us of what life was like for cowboys in the Old West. Men and women try to win prizes at a rodeo. They can choose to be in many kinds of _____ . Some people like to ride a wild horse or a bull. Others like to rope a calf or throw a steer onto its back.

1. The word that best completes the sentence is
   Ⓐ grass.　　Ⓑ islands.　　Ⓒ contests.

The wart hog is a type of pig that lives in Africa. The wart hog is a light gray color. It has short, stiff hairs on its body. It also has a _____ of longer hair that runs down its neck. The hog has a large head that is flat in front. It has long, curved teeth, or tusks. The hog gets its name from the three pairs of bumps called warts, on its head.

2. The word that best completes the sentence is
   Ⓐ basket.　　Ⓑ mane.　　Ⓒ party.

Long ago, people rushed west to hunt for gold. They lived in _____ near gold mines. Then they built homes. Soon whole towns grew up near the mines. But many of these towns didn't last long. When people had found all of the gold, they went to a new place. The towns they left behind became ghost towns. Only the empty buildings and streets were left.

3. The word that best completes the sentence is
   Ⓐ camps.　　Ⓑ chairs.　　Ⓒ dollars.

The day lily is a plant. It has _____ without leaves. At the end of each one is a group of flowers. These flowers are yellow or orange. During the summer, two or three of them bloom each day. They bloom when the sun comes up. Then they die when the sun sets.

4. The word that best completes the sentence is
   Ⓐ fences.　　Ⓑ apartments.　　Ⓒ stalks.

Name _____   Date _____

Lesson 6

≋ **Darken the circle for the answer that best completes the sentence.**

A cat's tongue feels rough. This is true for all cats. House cats, lions, and tigers all have rough tongues. A cat uses its tongue in many ways. It _____ itself to brush its fur. The cat removes dirt and loose hair this way. The cat also uses its rough tongue to scrape meat from a bone. When the cat is through, the bone is clean.

1. The word that best completes the sentence is
   Ⓐ paints.   Ⓑ licks.   Ⓒ frightens.

Trees are important. People make many things from trees. Trees are also helpful. They hold the dirt in place and help make the air we breathe. Trees are also the home for many creatures. So we need to be sure we _____ the trees. When old trees are cut down, new ones must be planted.

2. The word that best completes the sentence is
   Ⓐ forget.   Ⓑ find.   Ⓒ save.

Young people can join the 4-H Club. The goal of this club is to improve head, heart, hands, and health. Members have a chance to learn skills. They also find out about careers. Members try out jobs by working on _____. These jobs might deal with plants, animals, food, or safety.

3. The word that best completes the sentence is
   Ⓐ ice.   Ⓑ moments.   Ⓒ projects.

A barnyard pig takes a bath in mud. This is not because it likes to be dirty. In fact, it would like cool, clean water much better. But a pig must find a way to cool off. It can't _____ to stay cool the way people do. So it will lie in the mud to stay cool. The thick mud also helps the pig's skin. Insects can't bite it, and the sun won't burn it.

4. The word that best completes the sentence is
   Ⓐ fly.   Ⓑ sweat.   Ⓒ kick.

Name _____   Date _____

≋ **Darken the circle for the answer that best completes the sentence.**

Many travelers like to visit Birdhouse City. They can stay in one of the hotels. Or they might stay in the library or the church! These visitors aren't people who live in a small town. The people who live in the town made almost a hundred birdhouses. Most of the birdhouses look just like _____ in the real town. These houses make up Birdhouse City.

1. The word that best completes the sentence is
Ⓐ buildings.   Ⓑ friends.   Ⓒ cars.

Cedo is a monkey. He is the pet of a farm family. He likes to help out on the farm. He helps feed the _____ and load hay into the truck. He even drives the tractor! His owner never makes Cedo work. Cedo works because he thinks it is fun.

2. The word that best completes the sentence is
Ⓐ berries.   Ⓑ fences.   Ⓒ cows.

Whales make strange and wonderful _____ that sound like singing. These animals have more than one song. Whales in a group sing the same song for a while. Then they all sing another song. People don't know why whales sing. But they think it may be a kind of talking.

3. The word that best completes the sentence is
Ⓐ fish.   Ⓑ noises.   Ⓒ smiles.

A coconut makes a good toothbrush for an elephant. A person who works with an elephant may rub its teeth with a coconut. This doesn't _____ the elephant. It helps the elephant to stay healthy.

4. The word that best completes the sentence is
Ⓐ touch.   Ⓑ hurt.   Ⓒ show.

Name _____   Date _____

Lesson 8

≋ **Darken the circle for the answer that best completes the sentence.**

A dust devil is a fast-moving wind. It has dust or sand in it. It starts when hot air rises. The hot air begins to spin. It picks up dust or sand. The spinning _____ of air can stretch more than one thousand feet up into the sky.

1. The word that best completes the sentence is
   Ⓐ street.   Ⓑ column.   Ⓒ feet.

A peacock is a large bird. The male has very pretty tail feathers. The tail is big. It opens like a fan. It is full of bright colors. The feathers shine in the light of the sun. A male peacock will show his tail feathers to scare away other males. At other times, he will show his tail feathers to make a _____ peacock notice him.

2. The word that best completes the sentence is
   Ⓐ red.   Ⓑ female.   Ⓒ cold.

Donkey races are held in Colorado. The races honor the donkeys that carried packs for miners long ago. In the races, people run behind their donkeys. They guide them with ropes. The donkeys wear packs. The packs hold pans, picks, and _____. These were the miners' tools. The winner gets a cash prize.

3. The word that best completes the sentence is
   Ⓐ ovens.   Ⓑ airplanes.   Ⓒ shovels.

Every _____ you can watch the sun go down. At times the sun looks as if it is being flattened as it sets. But your eyes are being fooled. This happens when the rays of the light pass through Earth's air. The air right above Earth is cooler and thicker than the air higher up. This causes the rays of light to bend. The bent light makes the sun look flatter.

4. The word that best completes the sentence is
   Ⓐ evening.   Ⓑ morning.   Ⓒ hour.

Name _____ Date _____

≋ **Darken the circle for the answer that best completes the sentence.**

Some snakes have four eyes. They have eyes that see in the day. But they also have two more eyes. These eyes can see heat. Snakes use these eyes to look for food. A snake **gazes** all around with its special eyes. Its eyes cannot see a plant. Plants do not give off any heat. But the eyes can see a mouse. A mouse is warm and good for snakes to eat.

1. In this story, the word **gazes** means
Ⓐ stares.　　Ⓑ gives.　　Ⓒ adds.

Deep inside, the earth is made of very hot rock. The rock is so hot that it can turn water into steam. In some places, this steam comes out of cracks in the ground. In other places, people pipe the steam up from deep in the ground. People use this steam **energy** to warm their homes.

2. In this story, the word **energy** means
Ⓐ ice.　　Ⓑ power.　　Ⓒ stream.

What is vegetable art? Ask Bob Spohn. For fifty years Spohn has **whittled** faces and animals out of large vegetables. He uses a knife to make the faces. Then he paints them. He once made a smiling face from a giant pumpkin. The pumpkin was almost a yard high and weighed 110 pounds!

3. In this story, the word **whittled** means
Ⓐ drawn.　　Ⓑ shaken.　　Ⓒ cut.

You spill a drink on your clothes. What do you do? First find some club soda. Rub it on your clothes where the **stain** is. Dry your clothes with a towel. The spot should be gone.

4. In this story, the word **stain** means
Ⓐ mark.　　Ⓑ button.　　Ⓒ machine.

Lesson 10

≋ **Darken the circle for the answer that best completes the sentence.**

Bluebirds are pretty birds. Their head and wings are bright blue. Most bluebirds have some red on their chest. The bluebird's song is sweet. People are worried about this small bird. There used to be many of them in towns and forests. Now bluebirds are becoming very **rare**.

1. In this story, the word **rare** means
   Ⓐ hard to find.   Ⓑ mean.   Ⓒ fun to catch.

Most people think sea birds live only near the sea. But **numerous** sea birds fly toward land, too. In the spring and summer, they go to rivers and lakes to nest. They go to the same place every year.

2. In this story, the word **numerous** means
   Ⓐ troubled.   Ⓑ sick.   Ⓒ many.

Itzhak Perlman is a great violin player. As a boy he heard beautiful music on the radio. When he was just three years old, he **requested** a violin. He wanted to play beautiful music, too. At first his parents bought him a toy violin. But he knew it did not sound right. So they bought him a real one. Now he plays the violin all over the world.

3. In this story, the word **requested** means
   Ⓐ took away.   Ⓑ asked for.   Ⓒ got back.

There is a bird that can swim underwater and climb trees. It has claws on its wings. These birds build their nests over rivers and lakes. Sometimes the baby birds are afraid of other animals. Then they dive into the water and swim to another tree. They use their wing claws to climb up to a high branch. These birds use many tricks to **outwit** their enemies.

4. In this story, the word **outwit** means
   Ⓐ corner.   Ⓑ attack.   Ⓒ fool.

Lesson 11

≋ **Darken the circle for the answer that best completes the sentence.**

You may not know Clara Barton's name. You know her work, though. She started the American Red Cross. During the Civil War, Barton went to battles to help wounded soldiers. After the war, she saw that many soldiers could not find their families. She started to **trace** the missing people. Later she learned about the Red Cross in Europe. She decided that the United States needed a Red Cross, too.

1. In this story, the word **trace** means
Ⓐ mail.   Ⓑ teach.   Ⓒ find.

In the ocean, waves look like moving mountains. But when they get close to a beach, they begin to fall over. Why does this happen? Close to the shore the water is **shallow**. The waves that come from the deep sea are very tall. Then they get close to shore. They try to stand tall, but they fall over.

2. In this story, the word **shallow** means
Ⓐ not slow.   Ⓑ not deep.   Ⓒ not salty.

Benny Goodman was a bandleader. He was called the King of Swing. His band played music that had a new sound. This swing music was **snappy**. It had a strong beat. People danced a fast new dance to this music. It was also called the swing.

3. In this story, the word **snappy** means
Ⓐ tall.   Ⓑ gray.   Ⓒ quick.

Not all sharks are dangerous. Nurse sharks look dangerous, but they almost never hurt people. Instead they stay on the bottom of the ocean. They swim along, **sucking** in sand, crabs, snails, and tiny fish. They spit out the sand and eat the animals!

4. In this story, the word **sucking** means
Ⓐ rolling.   Ⓑ pulling.   Ⓒ calling.

Name _____ Date _____

≈ **Darken the circle for the answer that best completes the sentence.**

The first jigsaw puzzle was made in England. It was made by a teacher. The teacher wanted his students to learn about the map of England. He **glued** a map to a sheet of wood. Then he cut the map along county lines. The students loved working the puzzle. They learned all about the map of England.

1. In this story, the word **glued** means
   - Ⓐ served.
   - Ⓑ dressed.
   - Ⓒ pasted.

Squanto was a Native American. He was taken to Spain as a slave. But he ran away to England. Then Squanto sailed back to his home. He met the Pilgrims living at Plymouth. They were **nearly** dead. They had no food. Squanto helped the Pilgrims. He taught them how to plant corn. He showed them where to fish and hunt.

2. In this story, the word **nearly** means
   - Ⓐ tomorrow.
   - Ⓑ almost.
   - Ⓒ soon.

Most wild animals have color in their fur or skin. But some do not. These animals are called albinos. They are white or very **pale**. Their white color makes them easy to see. Albinos can't sneak up on smaller animals. They also can't hide. So they often die or become food for others.

3. In this story, the word **pale** means
   - Ⓐ light.
   - Ⓑ dark.
   - Ⓒ happy.

Neon is a type of gas found in the air. It is used in some **lamps** for homes and businesses. It is used to fill tubes for store signs, too. Now artists have found a new way to use neon. They make pictures with the neon-filled tubes. When the pictures are done, they are plugged in. People are amazed by the bright colors in neon art.

4. In this story, the word **lamps** means
   - Ⓐ barns.
   - Ⓑ coats.
   - Ⓒ lights.

Name _____ Date _____

≋ **Darken the circle for the answer that best completes the sentence.**

You may not see many wild animals during the day. But there is a way to tell where wild animals have been. You can look for their tracks. Tracks are the prints their feet leave on the ground. You can **determine** which wild creatures left the tracks. The size and shape of the tracks will give you clues.

1. In this story, the word **determine** means
  Ⓐ speak.　　　Ⓑ repair.　　　Ⓒ tell.

Waves often wash pretty shells up on the beach. But shells are not the only **appealing** things the waves bring. Sea beans are also washed up on shore. They are seeds and fruits from distant lands. They can be found on the beach from late March through the first part of summer.

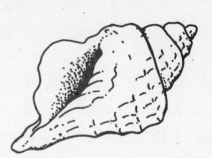

2. In this story, the word **appealing** means
  Ⓐ brave.　　·Ⓑ interesting.　　Ⓒ ugly.

Maya Lin drew a design for a contest. Her design won and was built. Thousands of names were carved on two walls of shiny, black stone. The names were Americans who had died in the Vietnam War. At first people thought that the stone was ugly. They **disliked** it. But then they began to change their minds. They found that they could walk up to the walls. They could touch the names of loved ones.

3. In this story, the word **disliked** means
  Ⓐ lost.　　　Ⓑ tricked.　　　Ⓒ hated.

Bobwhites are birds that live in groups. They search for insects and seeds in the woods. If the bobwhites come to a **clearing**, they run across it. They want to get back to the safety of the woods as fast as they can. At night these birds form a circle before they go to sleep. This helps them stay warm. They can also fly off in all directions if there's any danger.

4. In this story, the word **clearing** means
  Ⓐ river.　　　Ⓑ field.　　·Ⓒ mountain.

65

Lesson 14

≋ **Darken the circle for the answer that best completes the sentence.**

Roller-coaster cars are hooked to a chain at first. A motor on the ground runs the chain. It pulls the cars to the top of the first hill. Then the cars are unhooked. When the cars roll downhill, they speed up. The cars slow down as they **coast** up the next hill. They speed up again as they go down it. Each hill is a bit lower than the last. The cars can't go up a hill that is as high as the one they just came down.

1. In this story, the word **coast** means
Ⓐ move.   Ⓑ park.   Ⓒ leak.

Stevie Wonder was born blind. This did not stop him from using his talent. He found that he was good with music. He learned how to play many instruments. He wrote his own songs. At the age of twelve, he sang his first hit. Since then he has made many **albums**. He has even written music for a movie.

2. In this story, the word **albums** means
Ⓐ oranges.   Ⓑ buttons.   Ⓒ CDs.

Some people tell stories about Bunyips. Bunyips are said to live in lakes and rivers. There are many kinds of these strange beasts. Some are part person and part fish. Others look like big, brown creatures. They are **shaggy** and have big mouths. Still others look like dogs with webbed feet.

3. In this story, the word **shaggy** means
Ⓐ hairy.   Ⓑ silly.   Ⓒ empty.

The Great Salt Lake is in Utah. It used to be large. But it gets smaller each year. Homes that people built on the shore are now far from the water. This has happened because it is so hot and dry. The water dries up or **soaks** into the ground. There's not enough fresh water to make up for this loss.

4. In this story, the word **soaks** means
Ⓐ feels.   Ⓑ sinks.   Ⓒ ties.

Lesson 15

≋ **Darken the circle for the answer that best completes the sentence.**

A volcano blew up in Italy long ago. Some towns were covered by rivers of melted rock. One town was covered by 66 feet of hot black rock. It happened in just a few minutes. The towns were hidden under the rock for hundreds of years. When people found them again, they looked just as they had looked long ago. The towns were **preserved** by the rock.

1. In this story, the word **preserved** means
  Ⓐ tricked.   Ⓑ moved.   Ⓒ kept the same.

Some paintings are pictures of fruit or people. But some paintings are pictures of colors and shapes. These paintings **represent** ideas instead of things. A yellow line could remind us of anger. A red circle could remind us of love.

2. In this story, the word **represent** means
  Ⓐ cover up.   Ⓑ stand for.   Ⓒ step on.

A waterfall is noisy. It roars. It sprays your face if you get too close. It may drop hundreds of feet and crash onto rocks. The tallest waterfall in the world is Angel Falls. It is in a South American rain forest. The waters of Angel Falls **plunge** more than 3,000 feet.

3. In this story, the word **plunge** means
  Ⓐ drop.   Ⓑ break.   Ⓒ climb.

One bird really can swim like a fish. It is called the loon. This bird has been found more than one hundred feet below the water's **surface**. The bird can also fly. But it cannot walk. Its legs are very far back on its body. When it tries to stand up, it falls over.

4. In this story, the word **surface** means
  Ⓐ hole.   Ⓑ top.   Ⓒ ribbon.

Lesson 16

≋ **Darken the circle for the answer that best completes the sentence.**

Spanish explorers came to America long ago. They brought horses with them. Some of these horses got loose and **escaped**. Over the years, the number of wild horses grew. They became known as mustangs. Today there are still some herds of wild mustangs. They live in the West.

1. In this story, the word **escaped** means
   Ⓐ found.   Ⓑ ran away.   Ⓒ hurt.

The South Pole is the coldest place on earth. It's in the middle of Antarctica. The snow at the South Pole is more than a mile deep. But very little snow falls there. It snows far less than an inch each year. The little bit of snow that does fall can't melt. It lies on top of a solid layer of ice. For over a million years, the snow has **pressed** together to form this ice.

2. In this story, the word **pressed** means
   Ⓐ pushed.   Ⓑ hopped.   Ⓒ emptied.

The star-nosed mole has 22 feelers at the end of its nose. It hunts for food in ponds. When it **seizes** worms and tadpoles, the mole takes the food back to its hole. There it eats them.

3. In this story, the word **seizes** means
   Ⓐ hides.   Ⓑ cooks.   Ⓒ catches.

The sap from a poison ivy plant causes itchy bumps on your skin. It is best to know what this plant looks like. Poison ivy grows as a vine or shrub. The leaves are always in groups of three on each stem. But the color, size, and shape of the leaves can be different for each plant. Poison ivy **blooms** in the first part of summer. It has small blossoms that turn into berries.

4. In this story, the word **blooms** means
   Ⓐ flowers.   Ⓑ cries.   Ⓒ travels.

Exploring Comprehension Skills 3, SV 9781419030918

Unit 3

Writing

≋ **Read the sentences. Choose a word from the box to complete each one. Write the word on the line.**

joke	afternoon	glass	feed	leaves

1. It rained all _____.

2. The _____ on the trees turn red in the fall.

3. We _____ our pets every day.

4. Please pour me a _____ of milk.

5. Your funny _____ made me laugh.

≋ **Read each story. Write a word on each line that makes sense in the story.**

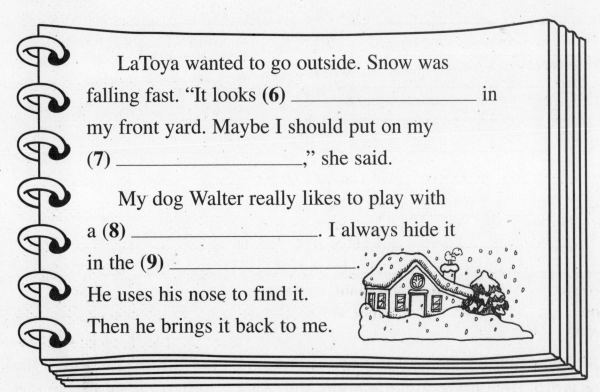

    LaToya wanted to go outside. Snow was falling fast. "It looks (**6**) _____ in my front yard. Maybe I should put on my (**7**) _____," she said.

    My dog Walter really likes to play with a (**8**) _____. I always hide it in the (**9**) _____. He uses his nose to find it. Then he brings it back to me.

GO ON →

Exploring Comprehension Skills 3, SV 9781419030918

Name _____ Date _____

Prewriting

≈ **Look through a book. Find a word that you do not know. Write the word on the chart. Write the sentence that you found. Then complete the rest of the chart.**

Word	Sentence
_____	_____ _____ _____
What I think the word means _____ _____ _____ _____ _____ _____ _____	**The definition I found** _____ _____ _____ _____ _____ _____ _____

On Your Own

≈ **Now use another sheet of paper. Write a short paragraph that uses the new word. Be sure to include clues that give a hint about the meaning of the word.**

Exploring Comprehension Skills 3, SV 9781419030918

Name _____ Date _____

What Is a Main Idea?

The main idea of a story tells what the whole story is about. Each story in this unit has a main idea. It is usually one sentence somewhere in each story.

Why do stories have sentences other than the main idea sentence? The other sentences are *details*. They tell you more about the main idea. They also make the story more fun to read.

The example below may help you think about main ideas. All the details add up to the main idea.

$$3 \quad + \quad 4 \quad + \quad 5 \quad = \quad 12$$
$$\text{detail} \; + \; \text{detail} \; + \; \text{detail} \; = \; \text{main idea}$$

The *3*, *4*, and *5* are like details. They are smaller than their sum, *12*. The *12*, like the main idea, is bigger. It is made up of many smaller parts.

Try It!

≈ **Read the story below. Draw a line under the main idea.**

> Do you sing in the bathtub? Do you sing in the car? Here's how you can become a singing star! You can go to a store. Someone will play music while you sing a song. Then the people there will make a recording of your song. You can take it home and surprise your friends!

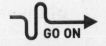

www.harcourtschoolsupply.com
© Harcourt Achieve Inc. All rights reserved.

71

Unit 4: What Is a Main Idea?
Exploring Comprehension Skills 3, SV 9781419030918

How to Choose a Main Idea

The main idea of the story is the sentence about becoming a singing star. All the other sentences are details. They tell how you can become a star. Write the details on the lines below.

Detail 1: You might sing in the _____ or in the

_____.

Detail 2: You can go to a _____.

Detail 3: Someone will play _____.

Detail 4: The people will make a _____ of your song.

Detail 5: You can _____ your friends.

Now write the main idea on the lines below. It is the sentence that is not a detail.

Main Idea: _____

_____

For Detail 1, you should answer *bathtub* or *car*. For Detail 2, you should answer *store*. For Detail 3, you should answer *music while you sing a song*. For Detail 4, you should answer *recording*. For Detail 5, you should answer *take it home and surprise*. The main idea is *Here's how you can become a singing star!*

- What do all the sentences add up to? Remember that the main idea is bigger than the details. It is made up of many smaller parts.

- Read each story. As you read, think about each sentence. Does it tell only a small part of the whole story? If it does, it is a detail. Does it tell what the story is about? Then it is the main idea.

Name _____ Date _____

≋ **Darken the circle for the answer that best completes the sentence.**

We make sounds by changing the shape of our mouth and throat. Do birds sing this way? Most people did not think so. But scientists have learned that birds sing different notes by changing the shape of their throat. It seems as if they sing like people.

1. The story mainly tells
   Ⓐ how people and birds sing.
   Ⓑ who uses air to make words.
   Ⓒ why people like to sing.

Howard was a shy little turtle. He was afraid to talk to anyone. He would always hide in his shell when new turtles came around. He pulled in his head and legs. He spent a lot of time inside his shell! Howard's mother wanted to help. She took him places where he would meet new turtles. Soon Howard got used to seeing lots of different people. He didn't hide in his shell anymore.

2. The story mainly tells
   Ⓐ why a turtle hid in his shell.
   Ⓑ how a turtle learned to not to be shy.
   Ⓒ how turtles play with others.

People who fish and people who like turtles are fighting. Some people like to catch fish with nets. But some sea turtles get stuck in the nets and die. Turtle lovers want fishing with nets to be against the law. They want people to fish with a new trap. The trap lets the turtles out but keeps the fish in. People who fish don't like the trap. They say that too many fish get out. They think the trap costs them too much money.

3. The story mainly tells
   Ⓐ why people are fighting over net fishing.
   Ⓑ which turtles get stuck in the nets.
   Ⓒ how much the fish traps cost.

Lesson 2

≋ **Darken the circle for the answer that best completes the sentence.**

There are many colors in the world. All colors are made from a mixture of three colors. These colors are blue, yellow, and red. They are called primary colors. Mix blue and red, and it will make purple. Blue and yellow will give you green. To make orange, mix red and yellow. Black is a mixture of blue, yellow, and red.

1. The story mainly tells
   Ⓐ about the way to make red.
   Ⓑ how all colors are made from primary colors.
   Ⓒ which colors to mix to make yellow.

Ezra Jack Keats wrote the book *The Snowy Day*. He painted all the pictures in it. Keats taught himself to paint. Keats started painting when he was four. As a child he painted on a metal table. He would cover it with pictures. His mother showed them to her friends before cleaning up the table.

2. The story mainly tells
   Ⓐ about Keats's life as a painter.
   Ⓑ that Keats painted on a board.
   Ⓒ that Keats didn't have paper for painting.

Long ago, people used their bodies to measure things. The first finger was used for small things. The width of that finger was a *digit*. A *span* was the width of a hand stretched out. A *cubit* was used to measure larger things. It was the length from the elbow to the tip of the longest finger.

3. The story mainly tells
   Ⓐ how the body was used for measuring things.
   Ⓑ that a *cubit* measured small things.
   Ⓒ what was measured with a *digit*.

A mosaic is a picture that is made from small pieces of stone or glass. The pieces are brightly colored. They are arranged to make a picture. The pieces are pressed into soft plaster. After the plaster hardens, a mosaic is made. Mosaics are used to decorate floors and walls.

4. The story mainly tells
   Ⓐ how fast plaster hardens.
   Ⓑ what kinds of pictures a mosaic can show.
   Ⓒ how a mosaic is made.

Name _____   Date _____

≋ **Darken the circle for the answer that best completes the sentence.**

Penguins are birds. But they cannot fly. They use their wings in other ways. They use them for swimming. Their wings are like flippers. In the summer they stay cool by holding their wings away from their bodies. Their wings are put to good use even if they cannot fly.

1. The story mainly tells
   Ⓐ where penguins live.
   Ⓑ how penguins use their wings.
   Ⓒ how penguins stay warm.

The Eiffel Tower is a big tower found in Paris, France. A man named Eiffel designed it for a fair. It is made of steel. It is more than 980 feet high. It weighs more than 7,000 tons. There are 1,652 steps to the top of the tower.

2. The story mainly tells
   Ⓐ what the Eiffel Tower is like.
   Ⓑ how many towers there are in France.
   Ⓒ how the Eiffel Tower is used.

A junk is a kind of boat. Junks sail on the seas of China and Southeast Asia. The sails of a junk have four sides. They are stretched over pieces of wood. Junks are used for fishing. Hong Kong is a very crowded city. So some people even live on their junks. A junk is sometimes a home for more than one family.

3. The story mainly tells
   Ⓐ where most people in Hong Kong live.
   Ⓑ about a boat called a junk.
   Ⓒ what junks are made of.

Emma Lazarus was a poet. She believed that America was the "land of the free." She knew that Jewish people were not treated fairly in many countries. She wanted to help them. So she wrote a poem. It is found on the Statue of Liberty. The statue and her famous poem greet the people who come to America.

4. The story mainly tells
   Ⓐ that Lazarus built the Statue of Liberty.
   Ⓑ that Lazarus didn't want to help people.
   Ⓒ that Lazarus wrote about freedom.

Name _____   Date _____

≋ **Darken the circle for the answer that best completes the sentence.**

Many people think sleet and freezing rain are the same thing. But they are not. Sleet is frozen raindrops. Freezing rain is liquid raindrops. Freezing rain does not turn to ice until it hits the ground. Sleet does not stick to trees or wires. But freezing rain does stick to both.

1. The story mainly tells
   Ⓐ that sleet sticks to trees and wires.
   Ⓑ that sleet and freezing rain are not the same.
   Ⓒ that freezing rain is more common than sleet.

When a star dies, a black hole may form. There is strong gravity in a black hole. Anything pulled inside the hole is twisted and stretched. Light is pulled into the hole. But light cannot get out. That is why it's called a black hole.

2. The story mainly tells
   Ⓐ about strong gravity.
   Ⓑ how a star dies.
   Ⓒ what a black hole is.

Porcupines like to eat salty things. A park ranger left his car window down. Sweat from the ranger's hands had coated the steering wheel. Sweat is salty. So what do you think happened? A porcupine ate the steering wheel!

3. The story mainly tells
   Ⓐ how a steering wheel got salty.
   Ⓑ why the park ranger left his window open.
   Ⓒ that porcupines eat almost anything salty.

Winter had come almost overnight. The new snow was just right for making a snowman. Sam put on his snow pants, coat, hat, and mittens. He got a carrot and some raisins. Sam went outside and began to roll the snow into large balls. He stacked them on top of each other to make a snowman. He used the carrot for a nose. He used the raisins for the eyes and a mouth. Sam remembered that there was an old hat in the closet. He decided to get it to put it on his snowman.

4. The story mainly tells
   Ⓐ how Sam made a snowman.
   Ⓑ that it had snowed.
   Ⓒ what to wear in snowy weather.

Lesson 5

≋ **Darken the circle for the answer that best completes the sentence.**

The bristlecone pine tree is one of the oldest plants on Earth. Most pine trees live for about 250 years. The bristlecone pine can live more than 4,000 years. It is also one of the slowest-growing plants. One tree took 1,500 years to grow 15 feet.

1. The story mainly tells
   Ⓐ where bristlecone pine trees grow.
   Ⓑ about a kind of old tree that grows slowly.
   Ⓒ why pine trees don't live long.

Early settlers made drinks from herbs and weeds. They added yeast to the drinks. The yeast made the drinks fizz. Native Americans also made drinks. But they made drinks from roots and barks. Together the settlers and the Americans made a new drink. They mixed roots and barks with yeast. They invented the first root beer!

2. The story mainly tells
   Ⓐ how root beer was invented.
   Ⓑ about drinks that the settlers made.
   Ⓒ that yeast makes drinks fizz.

The first bus service began in 1662. Blaise Pascal owned the first buses. The buses ran in Paris, France. But his buses were not like buses today. Pascal's buses were pulled by horses. Each bus carried eight riders.

3. The story mainly tells
   Ⓐ that Pascal had only eight buses.
   Ⓑ about the first bus service.
   Ⓒ that bus service was slow in 1662.

A moon is not the same as a planet. A planet is a world that moves around the Sun. A moon is much smaller than a planet. It moves around a planet. All but 2 of our planets have moons. These are Venus and Mercury. Earth and Pluto each have 1 moon. Jupiter has 16 moons!

4. The story mainly tells
   Ⓐ that Earth has 2 moons.
   Ⓑ that most planets don't have moons.
   Ⓒ how a moon and a planet are different.

Lesson 6

≈ **Darken the circle for the answer that best completes the sentence.**

The first person went up into space more than thirty years ago. His name was Yuri Gagarin. He was Russian. His spacecraft was the *Vostok 1*. It circled Earth just one time. Gagarin was in space for less than two hours.

1. The story mainly tells
  Ⓐ about the first manned spaceflight.
  Ⓑ that *Vostok 1* was a planet.
  Ⓒ which American was first in space.

How are a toad and a frog different? A toad spends more time out of water than a frog. Its skin is duller, rougher, and drier. The legs of a toad are shorter, too. A toad cannot jump as far as a frog. A frog lays its eggs in a jelly-like mass. A toad lays its eggs in strings. It wraps the eggs around the stems of water plants.

2. The story mainly tells
  Ⓐ where a frog lays its eggs.
  Ⓑ how a frog and a toad are different.
  Ⓒ how far a toad can jump.

Sitting Bull was a Sioux leader. He didn't want his people to lose their lands. He told the tribes to join against the white settlers. That way they might keep their homeland. In 1876 some tribes camped near the Little Bighorn River. General Custer and his troops charged the group. Sitting Bull's men destroyed the troops. It was a great win for Native Americans.

3. The story mainly tells
  Ⓐ how Custer won the Battle of Little Bighorn.
  Ⓑ that Sitting Bull was a peaceful man.
  Ⓒ how Sitting Bull's words helped the Sioux.

Name _____ Date _____

Lesson 7

≋ **Darken the circle for the answer that best completes the sentence.**

A geyser is a spring that throws out jets of hot water and steam. One geyser is found in Yellowstone National Park. It is called Old Faithful. It got its name because it spouted once an hour. Since it was found, it has never stopped spouting. It was found in 1870!

1. The story mainly tells
   Ⓐ about the age of Old Faithful.
   Ⓑ what Yellowstone National Park looks like.
   Ⓒ about a geyser called Old Faithful.

One animal has a nose six feet long. That's as big as a tall person! This long-nosed animal is an elephant. An elephant's nose is called a trunk. It lets an elephant breathe and smell. An elephant sucks water with its trunk. Then it gives itself a shower. It also uses its trunk to put food in its mouth.

2. The story mainly tells
   Ⓐ about an animal with a very long nose.
   Ⓑ why an elephant's nose is called a trunk.
   Ⓒ how an elephant can give itself a shower.

The Statue of Liberty is one big woman! Her hand is 16 feet long. One of her fingers is 8 feet long. Her head is 17 feet high. And her eyes are 2 feet wide. Even her fingernails are huge. They are more than 12 inches across.

3. The story mainly tells
   Ⓐ how long some people's fingernails are.
   Ⓑ how big the Statue of Liberty is.
   Ⓒ who the tallest woman in the world is.

Curling began in Scotland. It was played 500 years ago. It is a fun sport. It is played by sweeping ice. Each player has a large stone and a broom. The stones have handles on them. They weigh 35 pounds each. The players slide the stones across the ice toward a target. They sweep the ice in front of the stones to make them travel farther.

4. The story mainly tells
   Ⓐ what a curling stone is made of.
   Ⓑ how the sport of curling is played.
   Ⓒ that curling is played in Texas.

Name _____ Date _____

≋ **Darken the circle for the answer that best completes the sentence.**

Did you know that the world's largest bird can't fly? Can you name the bird? It's an ostrich. Why can't it fly? It's too big. An ostrich can be more than 8 feet tall. It can weigh more than 330 pounds. It lives in the grasslands of Africa.

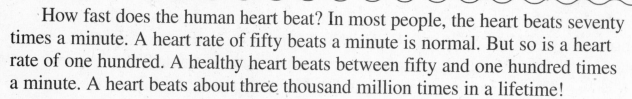

1. The story mainly tells
   Ⓐ which zoos have ostriches.
   Ⓑ about the largest bird in the world.
   Ⓒ how well ostriches hunt.

How fast does the human heart beat? In most people, the heart beats seventy times a minute. A heart rate of fifty beats a minute is normal. But so is a heart rate of one hundred. A healthy heart beats between fifty and one hundred times a minute. A heart beats about three thousand million times in a lifetime!

2. The story mainly tells
   Ⓐ about normal heart rates for humans.
   Ⓑ how to measure your heartbeat.
   Ⓒ about the heart rate during a heart attack.

There are eight notes on a musical scale. Each scale starts and ends with the same letter. One scale is C, D, E, F, G, A, B, C. From one C to the next C is called an octave. An *octave* is the eighth note of a scale. *Octave* comes from the Greek word *okto* meaning "eight."

3. The story mainly tells
   Ⓐ what a C note is.
   Ⓑ how many scales there are.
   Ⓒ what an octave is.

Julia Ward Howe wrote many poems and essays. She visited an army camp. She wrote a poem during her stay. It was "The Battle Hymn of the Republic." Later she set her poem to music. She used the tune from "John Brown's Body." "The Battle Hymn of the Republic" became the song of the Union army. It was sung during the Civil War.

4. The story mainly tells
   Ⓐ who wrote "John Brown's Body."
   Ⓑ who won the Civil War.
   Ⓒ about "The Battle Hymn of the Republic."

Name _____ Date _____

Lesson 9

≋ **Darken the circle for the answer that best completes the sentence.**

Jacques Cartier was a French explorer. He made three trips to Canada. Cartier tried to find out what the natives called their land. He asked a few of them. But they didn't understand him. They thought he was asking about their village. So they said, "Kanada." That was their word for *village*. So the huge country of Canada was named after a little village!

1. The story mainly tells
   Ⓐ which countries Cartier explored.
   Ⓑ how Canada was named after a village.
   Ⓒ that the natives didn't like Cartier.

There are many stories about King Arthur. He always met with his knights at a table. It was huge. It seated 150 people. At that time, the most important person sat at the head of a table. But King Arthur's table was round. So there wasn't any head of the table. All the seats were equal!

2. The story mainly tells
   Ⓐ how many knights King Arthur had.
   Ⓑ why King Arthur had a round table.
   Ⓒ that there are 150 stories about King Arthur.

Most fish lay eggs. Some fish leave their eggs to hatch by themselves. Other fish watch over their eggs. Mouthbrooders keep their eggs safe. They keep their eggs in their mouths. They even keep their young there. They can eat without swallowing any eggs or young!

3. The story mainly tells
   Ⓐ where most fish lay their eggs.
   Ⓑ how many eggs a mouthbrooder lays.
   Ⓒ about the safe place of a mouthbrooder.

George Herman Ruth liked to play baseball. His nickname was Babe. In 1914 he played for the Boston Red Sox. Ruth was just 19 years old. He played ball for 21 years. Why was he the king of home runs? Because he hit 714 home runs. His record was not broken for 40 years.

4. The story mainly tells
   Ⓐ what a great baseball player Ruth was.
   Ⓑ that George Ruth changed his name.
   Ⓒ that Ruth retired in 1935.

Unit 4: Main Idea, Lesson 9
Exploring Comprehension Skills 3, SV 9781419030918

Lesson 10

≋ **Darken the circle for the answer that best completes the sentence.**

Chopping an onion can make your eyes water. People try many things to keep from crying. Some people hold an onion under running water. Others try wearing goggles. But goggles make the cook look silly!

1. The story mainly tells
   - Ⓐ why onions make people cry.
   - Ⓑ ways to chop an onion without crying.
   - Ⓒ ways to use goggles.

The thigh bone is the biggest bone in the body. It connects the hip bone to the knee bone. Why does it need to be big and strong? It has to support the weight of the body. It must hold up the leg muscles, too. It needs to be long so that the legs can take wide steps.

2. The story mainly tells
   - Ⓐ that the biggest bone is found in the arm.
   - Ⓑ why the thigh bone is so big.
   - Ⓒ how bones help a person walk.

Milly the mouse ran into the kitchen. Just as she reached the table, Jep the cat crawled out from behind the washing machine. Milly needed to get away. She climbed up a table leg and hid under a plate. Jep looked all over the table. But he could not find Milly. Jep decided to wait for the mouse. He lay down under the table. Soon Jep was sleeping. Milly quietly ran back to her hole. "That was close!" she said.

3. The story mainly tells
   - Ⓐ why cats chase mice.
   - Ⓑ how animals hide.
   - Ⓒ how Milly escapes from Jep.

Name _____ Date _____

≈ **Darken the circle for the answer that best completes the sentence.**

What is the difference between a donkey and a mule? A donkey looks much like a horse. But it has long ears. It has a big head and a short mane. A donkey has two stripes on its back and shoulders. A mule has a horse for a mother and a donkey for a father. A mule is bigger than a donkey. It is stronger, too. But a mule is not as nervous as a donkey.

1. The story mainly tells
   Ⓐ how a donkey and a mule are different.
   Ⓑ that a donkey has shorter ears than a mule.
   Ⓒ that donkeys are bigger than mules.

The knife was an early invention. It was used for hunting and carving. In 1699 the King of France made a law about table knives. He ruled that table knives should have round ends. That would stop dinner guests from sticking each other. It would also stop people from picking their teeth with knives. Since then, table knives have had round ends.

2. The story mainly tells
   Ⓐ why table knives have round ends.
   Ⓑ that people still pick their teeth with knives.
   Ⓒ that the King of France invented the knife.

When a baby pelican is hungry, it looks for one of its parents. It taps on the parent's bill. The parent opens its mouth. The baby sticks its head inside. Fish that the parent has eaten come up. The baby feeds on this fish. The baby stays in the nest for ten weeks. It will weigh more than its parents. The young bird will live on the extra fat while it learns to catch fish.

3. The story mainly tells
   Ⓐ how pelicans catch fish.
   Ⓑ about baby pelicans.
   Ⓒ where pelicans build their nests.

Lesson 12

≈ **Darken the circle for the answer that best completes the sentence.**

Sometimes people can't remember their dreams. But everyone dreams while sleeping. Most people dream two hours every night. In that time they have four or five dreams. Each dream is longer than the dream before. You can tell when people are dreaming. Their eyeballs move back and forth under their closed eyelids.

1. The story mainly tells
   Ⓐ how much sleep people need.
   Ⓑ how often people dream.
   Ⓒ what dreams mean.

A snake doesn't open its mouth to stick out its tongue. The snake's jaw has a notch that lets the tongue move in and out. The tongue is not poisonous. It is used by the snake to smell. The tongue picks up air and carries it back into the mouth. There are two small holes on the roof of the mouth. It is these holes that smell the air.

2. The story mainly tells
   Ⓐ how a snake uses its tongue to smell.
   Ⓑ that a snake's tongue is poisonous.
   Ⓒ that a snake has three holes on its tongue.

Do you like bananas? Have you ever seen them growing outside? Bananas grow in bunches. A bunch of bananas is called a hand. Bananas grow in big hands. Each banana is called a finger. Each finger grows upward.

3. The story mainly tells
   Ⓐ how bananas grow.
   Ⓑ how to eat bananas with your fingers.
   Ⓒ how the banana got its name.

The fence-painting contest at Tom Sawyer Days is fun. Tom Sawyer is a boy from a well-known book. People dress up like Sawyer for the contest. They run toward a fence they must paint white. They have to paint it very fast. But they must paint it neatly. Most people finish it in about seven seconds!

4. The story mainly tells
   Ⓐ how to paint a fence.
   Ⓑ about a fence-painting contest.
   Ⓒ that Tom Sawyer was a painter.

Lesson 13

≋ **Darken the circle for the answer that best completes the sentence.**

Mother's Day comes in May. It is the second Sunday in May. It became a holiday in 1914. Who thought of Mother's Day? It was the idea of Anna May Jarvis. She wished she had been nicer to her mother in life. So she had a service in memory of her mother. She passed out flowers to all mothers who were there. People liked the thought of a day for mothers. In a few years, Mother's Day became a holiday in the United States.

1. The story mainly tells
   Ⓐ where Anna May Jarvis lived.
   Ⓑ about the month of May.
   Ⓒ about the start of Mother's Day.

There are big holes in the ground in some parts of the United States. But the holes weren't always there. They were formed after people looked for water. Water is found in big underground caves. People dig wells to reach it. As they pump the ground water out, the caves dry out. Sometimes when big trucks roll over an empty cave far below, the ground falls in. This leaves a big hole.

2. The story mainly tells
   Ⓐ what makes some holes in the ground.
   Ⓑ how caves become empty.
   Ⓒ how the water is pumped out.

Some ants live in trees. They bite through the wood and make nests and tunnels. Doors lead through the bark of the tree to the outside world. These ants keep out unwanted visitors by putting guards at the doors. Guards have heads like corks. They poke their heads out the door and stop up the hole.

3. The story mainly tells
   Ⓐ what kinds of trees ants live in.
   Ⓑ how some ants keep out visitors.
   Ⓒ how big the heads of ants are.

Harriet Quimby was a brave woman. The new idea of flying thrilled her. So she became a pilot in 1911. The next year she became the first woman to fly across the English Channel. That great flight showed how brave she was.

4. The story mainly tells
   Ⓐ how to be a pilot.
   Ⓑ about flying in 1911.
   Ⓒ about a brave woman pilot.

Exploring Comprehension Skills 3, SV 9781419030918

Name _____ Date _____

≈ **Darken the circle for the answer that best completes the sentence.**

The house sparrow is very common in many places around the world. Its beak is wide and short. It has small claws on its feet. It can live almost anywhere. House sparrows are found in cities and in the country.

1. The story mainly tells
   Ⓐ where sparrows live.
   Ⓑ what is strange about a sparrow.
   Ⓒ about a very common bird.

When pine cones are thrown into a campfire, they pop. The heat from the fire makes them pop open. When a forest is on fire, the pine cones in the trees pop. The seeds inside the cones scatter on the ground. That's why so many little pine trees grow quickly after a forest fire.

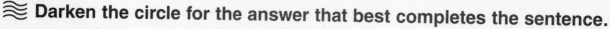

2. The story mainly tells
   Ⓐ why many new pine trees grow after a fire.
   Ⓑ that pine cones are used to build campfires.
   Ⓒ that pine cones cause forest fires.

Rosa Parks always took the bus home from work. The law at that time made African Americans sit in the back of buses. So Parks sat down in the back. The driver told her and three other people to give up their seats to white people. Parks refused. She was taken to jail. African Americans stopped riding buses. They thought the law was unfair. They worked to change the law. Today anyone can sit anywhere on a bus.

3. The story mainly tells
   Ⓐ about riding on a bus.
   Ⓑ how Parks helped change an unfair law.
   Ⓒ where Parks lived.

Newton was a pig. He wanted to be special. He decided to act differently. When his pig friends ate from a trough, Newton ate from a plate. When other pigs lay in the mud, Newton stayed in the shade. He did not want to get dirty. The other pigs did not think Newton was special. They did not want to play with him. Newton was lonely. He decided that he would rather have friends. Newton squealed with delight as he jumped into the mud.

4. The story mainly tells
   Ⓐ that Newton was not special.
   Ⓑ that Newton liked playing with his friends.
   Ⓒ that pigs like to play in the mud.

Lesson 15

≈ **Darken the circle for the answer that best completes the sentence.**

The white settlers thought bison were a kind of ox. So they called them bison, or buffalo. Bison were hunted for their hides. The hides kept people warm. Bison meat made good food, too. The bison tongue was a special treat. But soon the big herds became small herds. Few bison were left. They were put on special land. Today most bison live in protected herds.

1. The story mainly tells
   Ⓐ about bison.
   Ⓑ how bad bison tongue tasted.
   Ⓒ that bison hides kept people warm.

Willie Mays loved baseball. But he could not play in the major leagues. African Americans couldn't play with white players. Mays played in the Negro Leagues. Then the New York Giants hired Mays. Mays played very well. He became a big star. He hit 660 homeruns. Mays played with the Giants and the Mets. Today he is in the Baseball Hall of Fame.

2. The story mainly tells
   Ⓐ how long Mays played baseball.
   Ⓑ that Mays played for the Mets.
   Ⓒ that Mays was a great baseball player.

The fruit of the squirting cucumber looks like a little pickle. Its skin stretches as it grows. Pressure builds inside the fruit. When the fruit is ripe, it falls off the stem. This opens a hole at one end. The seeds squirt out from the hole. They can fly as far as 25 feet.

3. The story mainly tells
   Ⓐ about a fruit that squirts its seeds.
   Ⓑ about a kind of pickle.
   Ⓒ where cucumber seeds come from.

Name _____ Date _____

≈ **Darken the circle for the answer that best completes the sentence.**

Babies use both hands. But babies use one hand more than the other. This hand may become the preferred one. How can you tell? Lay a baby on its back. Notice which side the baby faces. It the baby looks to the right most of the time, it will probably be right-handed. What does it mean if the baby faces left more often? The baby will most likely be left-handed.

1. The story mainly tells
   Ⓐ how to tell right- from left-handed babies.
   Ⓑ that babies use their hands for many things.
   Ⓒ that there are more left-handed babies.

Do you ever wonder how you taste things? You owe your sense of taste to your taste buds. We have nine thousand taste buds just on the tongue alone. There are also taste buds on the roof of your mouth. You even have taste buds on the back of your throat.

2. The story mainly tells
   Ⓐ why we can taste only sweet things.
   Ⓑ that we taste through our nose.
   Ⓒ where taste buds are found.

Sand isn't as quiet as it may seem to be. It can make sounds. Sand whistles, squeaks, and booms. It whistles when someone walks on it. Try running on sand. You'll hear it squeak. It whistles and squeaks when a stick is jammed into it. Next time you are at the beach, build a sand castle. You'll hear it boom when it falls.

3. The story mainly tells
   Ⓐ that sand is quiet.
   Ⓑ where sand comes from.
   Ⓒ about the noises that sand makes.

Were you born after 1985? If so, how long do you expect to live? Most people born after 1985 can expect to live more than 70 years. Of course, this is just a guess based on past records. By the way, females can expect to live about six years longer than males. That's taken from past records, too!

4. The story mainly tells
   Ⓐ why people live to be 70.
   Ⓑ how long you might expect to live.
   Ⓒ about the health of females.

Unit 4

Writing

≈ **Read each story. Think about the main idea. Write the main idea in your own words.**

1. Most people think of the White House as the home of the President of the United States. But this was not always true. George Washington did not live in the White House. He lived in New York.

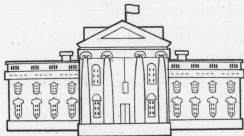

_____

_____

2. Farmers in Japan have a problem. There is not much land to farm, and there are many people to feed. Some farmers cut rows in the hillsides and grow crops there. This helps a little, but many kinds of food are shipped to Japan. They can choose anything they want to eat!

_____

_____

3. Paul Bunyan was a very tall man. He used his ax to cut down trees long ago in the West. He and his ox, Babe, would walk from forest to forest. His feet were so big, they pressed into the ground. When it rained, the footprints would fill with water and make lakes.

_____

_____

Prewriting

≋ Think of a main idea that you would like to write about, such as a place to go or an important person. Fill in the chart below.

Main Idea

Detail

Detail

On Your Own

≋ Now use another sheet of paper to write your story. Underline the sentence that tells the main idea.

Name _____ Date _____

What Is a Conclusion?

A conclusion is a decision you make after thinking about all the clues. A writer does not always tell you his or her conclusions. When you read, you have to hunt for clues. Then you must put all the clues together to draw a conclusion. This will help you understand the story.

The conclusions are not stated in the stories in this unit. You will have to read the stories. Then you will draw conclusions from what you have read.

Try It!

≈ **Read this story about whales. Think about the clues it gives you.**

A mother whale helps her baby take its first breath. She pushes the new baby up for air. The mother whale stays by her baby for about a year. She keeps the baby safe. She feeds it milk.

How to Draw a Conclusion

Look at the story about whales again. Look at the clues in the story. They will help you draw a conclusion about mother whales. Write the clues about mother whales on the lines. The first one has been done for you.

Clue 1: A mother whale *helps her baby take its first breath*.

Clue 2: A mother whale _____

_____.

Clue 3: A mother whale _____

_____.

Now try to draw a conclusion about whales. Do you think that whales take care of their babies?

Conclusion: Whales take _____

_____.

- Look at all the clues in the story. The first clue about the mother whale is that she helps her baby take its first breath. A second clue is that she keeps her baby safe. A third clue is that she feeds her baby milk.

- Look at all the clues together. If it helps, write the clues in your own words. Then make a decision about the story. Your decision will come from the clues. From the story about whales, you might decide that mother whales care for their babies. How do you know that? Mother whales help their babies breathe. They also give them safety and food.

Name _____   Date _____

≋ **Darken the circle for the answer that best completes the sentence.**

Barney stepped back to look at his work. He leaned his head to one side as he gazed at the canvas. Then he wiped his hands with a rag and cleaned all his brushes.

1. From this story, you can tell
   Ⓐ Barney is a painter.
   Ⓑ Barney is a cook.
   Ⓒ Barney is a dentist.

The phone rang. Mrs. Bond answered it and talked for some time to the caller. As she spoke, she played nervously with her hair. At one point she covered her eyes with her hand. When she got off the phone, Mrs. Bond sighed and went to the window. She stood there for a while, staring out but seeing nothing.

2. From this story, you can tell
   Ⓐ that the call was good news.
   Ⓑ that the call caused her to worry.
   Ⓒ that the call was from a friendly neighbor.

Mack awoke with a start and jumped out of bed. He realized that he had slept through the alarm again. Quickly he threw on his clothes and hunted for his socks and shoes. Minutes later Mack was flying down the street to the bus stop. At the bus stop, his feet felt funny. Something was wrong. When Mack looked down and saw what he had done, he shook his head and laughed.

3. From this story, you can tell
   Ⓐ Mack's socks were different colors.
   Ⓑ Mack's shoes were on the wrong feet.
   Ⓒ Mack forgot his coat.

A hungry wolf met a fat, well-fed dog. "Come home with me!" said the dog. "My master will feed you every day. All you have to do is wear a collar and follow orders." The wolf said, "Thanks anyway. I would rather go hungry but be free than be well fed and a slave."

4. From this story, you can tell
   Ⓐ the wolf did not need food.
   Ⓑ the owner was unkind to the dog.
   Ⓒ the wolf did not go home with the dog.

Lesson 2

≋ **Darken the circle for the answer that best completes the sentence.**

Without bees, some of our prettiest flowers would never bloom. Flowers make a special dust. A bee flies to different flowers and drinks the flower's sweet juice. As the bee drinks, it is covered with this dust. It carries the dust with it. At the next flower, the bee drinks again. The dust falls on special parts inside the flower. Then the plant can make seeds. The seeds become new plants.

1. From this story, you can tell
   Ⓐ the flowers and the bees need each other.
   Ⓑ bees are bad for most kinds of plants.
   Ⓒ bees do not like the dust that gets on them.

There were many factories in the city. The factories turned the air black with smoke. One morning there was a heavy fog. People began to have trouble breathing. Many people called their doctor or went to the hospital. Finally it rained, and the fog lifted. The people began to feel better. Without the fog, they could breathe easily again.

2. From this story, you can tell
   Ⓐ the doctors didn't have very much work.
   Ⓑ the people got sick from the smoke and fog.
   Ⓒ the rain sent many people to the hospital.

At one time, a cat that caught mice cost four days' pay. If you killed a cat, you had to give its owner a sheep and a lamb. Or you could pay with a pile of grain. To measure the grain, someone held the dead cat by its tail. Its nose touched the ground. Grain was poured out until the cat was covered. This pile of grain paid for the food that mice ate because the cat was not around.

3. From this story, you can tell
   Ⓐ a dead cat was worth more than a live one.
   Ⓑ kittens were better to have than cats.
   Ⓒ cats cost so much because they ate mice.

Name _____ Date _____

Lesson 3

≋ **Darken the circle for the answer that best completes the sentence.**

The homeless children were often tired and sick. Their skin was red.
The doctor wondered why the children were this way. The doctor thought
about the food he ate. He ate meat and drank milk. He almost
never got sick. He thought about the food that poor children
ate. It wasn't very healthy food. So the doctor decided to
feed meat and milk to the sick children. The children got
better very soon.

1. From this story, you can tell
   Ⓐ eating well helps people stay healthy.
   Ⓑ only children get sick.
   Ⓒ drinking milk makes people's skin red.

A company makes a machine that helps babies sleep. People can put the
machine on their baby's bed. The machine shakes the bed softly. The shaking
feels just like a ride in a car. The machine also makes noise. But this noise
sounds like the wind blowing against a car window.

2. From this story, you can tell
   Ⓐ babies like the sound of the ocean.
   Ⓑ babies don't like the machine very much.
   Ⓒ many babies sleep when they ride in cars.

"My garden! My corn!" Ellie cried. The garden looked awful. Most of the
corn plants were broken. Many ears of corn had been eaten. Some of the young
plants lay on the ground. Ellie looked at the ground that was still wet. It had
rained two days before. Then she spotted some tracks about two inches long.
The tracks led from the garden to the woods.

3. From this story, you can tell
   Ⓐ this was Ellie's first garden.
   Ⓑ the wind and rain broke the corn plants.
   Ⓒ there had been an animal in the garden.

Lesson 4

≈ **Darken the circle for the answer that best completes the sentence.**

Fred Gipson was a famous writer. As a boy he loved stories. Fred's grandfather told him many stories. Once Fred's grandfather told him about a big, yellow dog. This dog saved a man from a sick wolf. Later Fred wrote a book about this dog. The title of his book was *Old Yeller*.

1. From this story, you can tell
   Ⓐ Fred's book was about a yellow wolf.
   Ⓑ Fred used a story to write a book.
   Ⓒ Fred's book was about his grandfather.

Today most people eat with a knife, fork, and spoon. But people didn't always use these things. The knife is the oldest of the three. The first knives were made of stone. People have used some kind of knife for more than a million years. The first spoons were just scooped-out pieces of wood. People have used spoons for twenty thousand years. The fork came into use only five hundred years ago.

2. From this story, you can tell
   Ⓐ people have used forks longer than spoons.
   Ⓑ people have used spoons longer than forks.
   Ⓒ people have always used forks.

The longest cave in the world is Mammoth Cave. It is found in Flint Ridge, Kentucky. This cave runs under the ground for more than two hundred miles. The cave is full of strange things. There are many tall, limestone columns. There are lakes and even a river inside the cave. This river is called the Echo River. It runs almost four hundred feet under the ground.

3. From this story, you can tell
   Ⓐ Mammoth Cave is above the ground.
   Ⓑ it is fun to sail on the Echo River.
   Ⓒ a trip through the cave would take time.

Lesson 5

≈ **Darken the circle for the answer that best completes the sentence.**

Have you ever looked at a map of the United States? Many states have strange shapes. The bottom part of Michigan looks like a mitten. Maine looks like the head of a buffalo. Tennessee is shaped like a sled. Also, California looks like an arm. Try to remember these strange shapes. They will help you remember the states.

1. From this story, you can tell
  Ⓐ many states have different shapes.
  Ⓑ Maine has the shape of a mitten.
  Ⓒ the shapes will help you forget the states.

In Europe most people eat with the fork held in the left hand. Most Americans hold it in their right hand. Why is it different? In the pioneer days, there was not always enough food to eat. So people ate very fast. They could eat even faster by holding the fork in their right hand.

2. From this story, you can tell
  Ⓐ pioneers liked to eat slowly.
  Ⓑ everyone holds the fork in the left hand.
  Ⓒ Americans and Europeans eat differently.

The Germans had a special idea for birthday parties. The birthday cake always had candles on it. They would always put one more candle than the age of the child. So if the child was five, the cake had six candles. The extra candle stood for the "light of life." It was a wish for good health in the coming year.

3. From this story, you can tell
  Ⓐ the extra candle had a special meaning.
  Ⓑ the cake had more candles than frosting.
  Ⓒ the Germans did not like birthdays.

Lesson 6

≋ **Darken the circle for the answer that best completes the sentence.**

Today you can find buttons on many clothes. But buttons have not always been used to fasten clothes. Only belts and pins were used before to fasten parts of clothes. For hundreds of years, buttons were used like jewels. They were put on clothes just for their beauty. Finally in the 1200s, buttons were used as fasteners on clothes.

1. From this story, you can tell
   Ⓐ buttons are still used only for beauty.
   Ⓑ pins and belts are better than buttons.
   Ⓒ buttons are used as fasteners, along with belts and pins.

Marco Polo was a famous traveler. His home was in Venice, Italy. In 1271 he made a trip to the Far East. In China he became friends with the ruler. His name was Kublai Khan. Polo became his helper. He stayed in China for twenty years. Then he went back home. There he wrote a book. The book told all about the Far East.

2. From this story, you can tell
   Ⓐ Marco Polo got lost on his trip.
   Ⓑ Venice is west of China.
   Ⓒ Marco Polo did not stay long in China.

There are bugs that live under the ground for 17 years. As young bugs, they spend their time eating roots. Finally, in their seventeenth summer, they crawl up into the open air. They climb the trees and live for just a few weeks. Then they die. Everybody knows when these bugs come out. The males sing to their mates all day long. Sometimes their sound can even drown out airplane noise.

3. From this story, you can tell
   Ⓐ these bugs bite people.
   Ⓑ the males sing only at night.
   Ⓒ the bugs' sound is very loud.

Lesson 7

≈ **Darken the circle for the answer that best completes the sentence.**

Times change and so do prices. In the 1930s, you could go to the movies for ten cents. For that price you saw a movie and a cartoon! At that time one of the big movie stars was a little girl. Her name was Shirley Temple.

1. From this story, you can tell
   Ⓐ Shirley Temple is still a little girl.
   Ⓑ some things cost less in the 1930s.
   Ⓒ Temple's picture is found on a dime.

"Cooking is easy," Lisa said. "Who need lessons? I know what to do."

Lisa turned the stove on high. She put the ham over the hot flame. Jenny put some salt into the tea. Then she added water and let it boil. The girls also decided to make some bread.

"What about the lumps?" Lisa asked.

Jenny said, "Just hope that nobody notices, I guess."

By now the ham had burned. The teas tasted awful, too. So Lisa and Jenny had peanut butter sandwiches for dinner.

2. From this story, you can tell
   Ⓐ the girls tried to bake a cake.
   Ⓑ the girls have cooked for many years.
   Ⓒ the girls really need cooking lessons.

The albatross is a big bird. It lives near the sea. This bird can sometimes fly for six days without moving its wings. The albatross knows how to glide on airstreams. It has more wing feathers than other birds. This bird can even sleep while flying!

3. From this story, you can tell
   Ⓐ the albatross has a hidden motor.
   Ⓑ the albatross can fly very well.
   Ⓒ the albatross is a lazy bird.

Name _____   Date _____

Lesson 8

≈ **Darken the circle for the answer that best completes the sentence.**

Some towns in the United States have strange names. Many of these names are not English. Take Baton Rouge as an example. It's the capital of Louisiana. Its name comes from French words. *Baton rouge* means "red stick." Long ago, Native Americans used red sticks to mark off their hunting grounds. The French settlers named the town after these red sticks.

1. From this story, you can tell
   Ⓐ the names of towns are not always English.
   Ⓑ Baton Rouge is a French settler's name.
   Ⓒ Louisiana is part of England.

There are different ways to tell how hot or cold it is outside. But do you know a fun way to measure the heat? First you must listen for the cricket chirps. Then you need to count the chirps for 15 seconds. Then add 40 to the number of chirps. Your answer should be close to the real temperature.

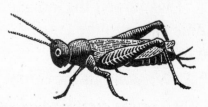

2. From this story, you can tell
   Ⓐ crickets chirp louder when it is cold.
   Ⓑ only crickets are used to measure the heat.
   Ⓒ crickets chirp faster as the heat rises.

Charles Blondin was a brave man. In 1859 he crossed Niagara Falls on a tightrope. Then he put on a blindfold and crossed the rushing water again. But that wasn't all he did. He walked the rope with stilts. As his last trick, he walked halfway across the tightrope. There he stopped for breakfast! He cooked some eggs and ate them. Then he made his way to the other side.

3. From this story, you can tell
   Ⓐ Blondin was a poor swimmer.
   Ⓑ Blondin was comfortable on the tightrope.
   Ⓒ Blondin was not afraid of water.

Lesson 9

≋ **Darken the circle for the answer that best completes the sentence.**

Big Bend is a very large park. It is found in West Texas. The park covers thousands of square miles. The park is full of mountains and canyons. The land is rough and rocky. There is a story that tells why Big Bend is this way. It goes back to when the earth was being made. The story says that the extra parts were dropped into Big Bend.

1. From this story, you can tell
   Ⓐ Big Bend is a clock.
   Ⓑ the park is found in West Virginia.
   Ⓒ why Big Bend is so rocky.

Whooping cough makes people very sick. Today it is cured with medicine. But four hundred years ago, people got rid of it in other ways. One way was to put a live frog in the sick person's mouth. Another way was to hold a spider near the sick person's head. Then the cough was told to go away.

2. From this story, you can tell
   Ⓐ ways to treat whooping cough have changed.
   Ⓑ frogs are a good cure for many things.
   Ⓒ a frog a day keeps the doctor away.

April 22 is known as Earth Day. On this day people honor our planet, Earth. Earth is our home. We must remember to take care of it. Earth Day is a good time for picking up litter. Cleaning a park is a good idea. But we should help our Earth every day.

3. From this story, you can tell
   Ⓐ Earth Day takes place in August.
   Ⓑ Earth sometimes needs help.
   Ⓒ we should not help clean up litter.

Lesson 10

≋ **Darken the circle for the answer that best completes the sentence.**

Tom Thumb was a famous circus star. His real name was Charles Stratton. As a grown-up, Thumb was just forty inches tall. In his circus act, Thumb had fights for fun with tall people. He sang, danced, and joked, too. Thumb had fans all over the world. He even met the Queen of England and Abraham Lincoln. Thumb did not let his small size trouble him. He once said, "I feel I am as big as anybody."

1. From this story, you can tell
   Ⓐ Thumb's small size made him famous.
   Ⓑ Abraham Lincoln acted in a circus.
   Ⓒ Thumb was no bigger than a thumb.

Some of the names of American states are French. For example, *Vermont* means "green mountain." Maine was named after a place in France. Louisiana was named after a French king.

2. From this story, you can tell
   Ⓐ Maine was named after a king.
   Ⓑ some states do not have English names.
   Ⓒ Louisiana is the name of a mountain.

Baseball is a fun game. Today many people play it. But long ago it was played in a different way. In the 1830s, baseball was called town ball. Big rocks were used as bases. The playing field was square. The pitcher was known as the feeder. The batter was called the striker. When the batter hit the ball, he ran clockwise around the bases. A fielder would throw the ball at the runner. If the ball hit the runner, he was out!

3. From this story, you can tell
   Ⓐ baseball was once called football.
   Ⓑ town ball used a round field.
   Ⓒ some baseball rules have changed.

Name _____ Date _____

Lesson 11

≈ **Darken the circle for the answer that best completes the sentence.**

Angel Falls is a waterfall in Venezuela. Venezuela is a country in South America. Angel Falls is the highest waterfall in the world. It is a part of the Churún River. Its waters drop more than half a mile. Angel Falls was named after an American. His name was Jim Angel. He found the waterfall while hunting for gold.

1. From this story, you can tell
   Ⓐ the Churún River is not very deep.
   Ⓑ Angel Falls is found on a mountain.
   Ⓒ Jim Angel found a gold mine.

Do you like peanuts? Many people do. In fact, March is known as Peanut Month. People in the United States eat many peanuts. They eat more than one billion pounds of peanuts a year. Half of this is eaten as peanut butter.

2. From this story, you can tell
   Ⓐ peanuts are a favorite American food.
   Ⓑ May is Peanut Month.
   Ⓒ peanut butter is made from walnuts.

The year was 1960. Chubby Checker was only 19 years old. Checker liked to dance. But he was tired of the same old dances. He wanted a new dance. So he made up a few new steps. The dance was called the Twist. He even wrote a song to go along with his new dance. Soon young people everywhere were doing the Twist.

3. From this story, you can tell
   Ⓐ people did not like Checker's new song.
   Ⓑ Checker never learned to dance.
   Ⓒ the Twist became a well-known dance.

Lesson 12

≋ **Darken the circle for the answer that best completes the sentence.**

Do you like pigs? Some people do. In fact, some people keep pigs as pets. Pigs are not really dirty animals. They really don't even smell bad. But they do like to roll around in the mud. This helps them keep cool. Did you know that pigs even have their own day? It's March 1, and it's called National Pig Day.

1. From this story, you can tell
   Ⓐ pigs hate mud.
   Ⓑ National Pig Day is in April.
   Ⓒ pigs can make good pets.

People once had to buy most of their food fresh. There were no frozen foods. Some foods were treated with salt to make them last longer. Vinegar was used to treat foods, too. Then in the 1920s, a man had an idea. His name was Charles Birdseye. His idea was to quick-freeze foods. His new idea was a success.

2. From this story, you can tell
   Ⓐ salt freezes foods.
   Ⓑ quick-freezing is a good way to store foods.
   Ⓒ vinegar made foods taste better.

Every year people invent strange things. Sometimes these things are of some use. Many times they are not. Eyeglasses for chickens are an example. Chickens like to peck at each other. So someone made a pair of eyeglasses for chickens to wear. They were strapped on the birds' heads. They were meant to protect the chickens' eyes!

3. From this story, you can tell
   Ⓐ the eyeglasses for chickens were of no use.
   Ⓑ the eyeglasses helped the chickens read.
   Ⓒ all chickens wear glasses today.

104

Lesson 13

≈ **Darken the circle for the answer that best completes the sentence.**

The most common illness is the cold. Some people say you should not go out in cold weather without a coat. They say you will catch a cold. This is not true. Colds are caused by viruses, not by cold weather. To keep from catching colds, you should wash your hands often.

1. From this story, you can tell
   Ⓐ cold weather causes colds.
   Ⓑ that wearing a coat can keep you from catching colds.
   Ⓒ washing your hands can help keep you from catching colds.

Many farmers use dogs to herd sheep. These dogs can be trained to do as they're told. One farmer kept his pigs and sheep together. He trained his dog to herd the sheep. But the farmer noticed that the sheep always followed the pigs. So he decided to use one of the pigs to herd the sheep. Now the farmer's dog is out of work. When the farmer wants the sheep to come, he calls, "Here, piggy, piggy!"

2. From this story, you can tell
   Ⓐ pigs can be useful on a farm.
   Ⓑ sheep are smart.
   Ⓒ pigs don't like sheep.

Tina answered the door. A man stood on the dark porch. "My car broke down," he said. I need to use your phone." He started to come into the house.

But Tina felt something was wrong. She quickly closed the door and locked it. "I'll call someone to help you," she yelled. But the man ran away. Later Tina heard that the man had robbed a neighbor.

3. From this story, you can tell
   Ⓐ Tina doesn't like to help anybody.
   Ⓑ the man really didn't have car trouble.
   Ⓒ the man wanted to sell something to Tina.

Name _____ Date _____

≈ **Darken the circle for the answer that best completes the sentence.**

When the whistle blows, everybody gets off the ice. The ice is bumpy and rough. Sharp skates have made cuts in it. A noisy machine moves around the rink like a fat duck. The machine makes the ice as smooth as glass. The machine was first built in California in 1942. Before 1942, it took two hours to smooth the ice. Three people did the job with shovels.

1. From this story, you can tell
   Ⓐ the machine makes a hard job much easier.
   Ⓑ four people can work as fast as the machine.
   Ⓒ three people push the machine on ice.

Without the sun, nothing could live on Earth. It would be too cold. But the sun won't last forever. Millions of years from now, the sun will stop shining. It will run out of gases to burn. When this happens, the sun will become very big. It will burn brightly for a short time. Then it will cool and become very small.

2. From this story, you can tell
   Ⓐ when the sun cools, it will become small.
   Ⓑ after the sun dies, Earth will live forever.
   Ⓒ someday the sun will turn bright blue.

George Goodale loved plants. He wanted to have some plants in his museum. But he didn't want just any old plants. Dried plants wouldn't look very nice. Wax plants would melt. Live plants would need too much care. So he used glass plants. Today, people can look at them in his museum. The berries look good enough to eat. The cactus plants have spines that look real. Each glass spine was made by hand.

3. From this story, you can tell
   Ⓐ glass plants look nicer than dried plants.
   Ⓑ glass plants change color in the sun.
   Ⓒ wax plants look as nice as glass plants.

Unit 5

Writing

≈ **Read the story. What conclusion can you draw? Use the clues in the story to answer the questions in complete sentences.**

Ana likes her Aunt Lynn. When Ana was a little girl, her aunt came to visit her. She read to Ana. In a way, Ana got her love of reading from Aunt Lynn. Now Aunt Lynn is older. Her eyes are not good. She still can see. But she can't see very much, and she can't read at all. So Ana visits her Aunt Lynn now. They talk to each other. After that, Ana reads to Aunt Lynn. Her aunt likes that.

1. Did Aunt Lynn live with Ana? How do you know?

_____

_____

2. Were Aunt Lynn's eyes always so weak? How do you know?

_____

_____

3. Does Ana make Aunt Lynn happy? How do you know?

_____

_____

GO ON →

107

Prewriting

≋ Think of a conclusion you can make about a person you know or something that you like to do. Write it in the conclusion box. Fill in the chart with some clues that could help another person make the same conclusion.

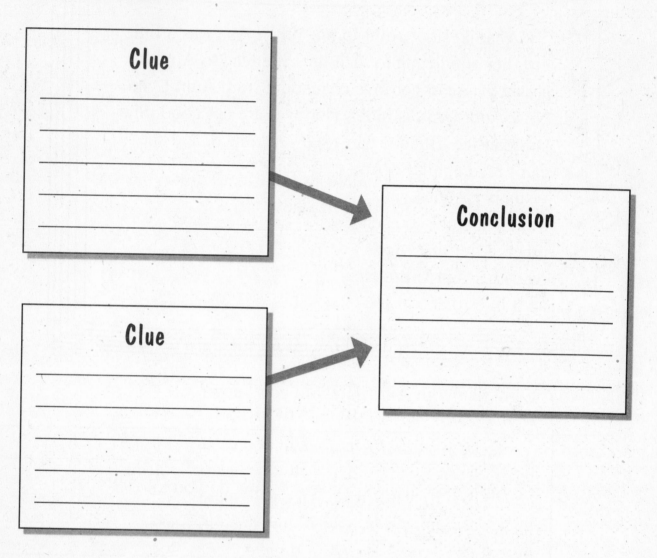

On Your Own

≋ Now use another sheet of paper to write a paragraph to describe the person you know or the thing you like to do. Do not state the conclusion. Just use the clues from above. Then trade papers with another student and write a conclusion using the clues.

Unit 6

What Is an Inference?

An inference is a guess you make after thinking about what you already know. For example, a friend invites you to a party. From what you know about parties, you might infer that there will be games, gifts, food, and drinks.

An author does not write every detail in a story. If every detail were told, stories would be long and boring. The main point would be lost. Suppose you read, "Pat went to the grocery store." The writer would not have to tell you what a grocery store is. The writer expects you to know that it is a place where people buy food. When you hear the words *grocery store*, you may think of long rows of shelves with canned foods. Or you may think of cases filled with cheese and milk. By filling in these missing details, you could infer that Pat went to the store to buy food. The writer expects you to infer the missing details from what you know.

Try It!

≈ **Read this story about Jacob. Think about the facts in the story.**

> ### Jacob's Morning
>
> Jacob walked down the hall at school. He pushed back his straight, red hair with one hand. He hadn't combed it. He rubbed his eyes with a fist. He hadn't washed his face. His shirt was wrinkled. One shoelace was untied. It dragged along the floor as he walked.

Exploring Comprehension Skills 3, SV 9781419030918

How to Make an Inference

Look at the story about Jacob again. Look at the facts in the story. They will help you make an inference about Jacob. Write the facts on the lines. The first one has been done for you.

Fact 1: Jacob had forgotten _____*to comb his hair*_____.

Fact 2: He hadn't _____.

Fact 3: His shirt _____.

Fact 4: One shoelace _____.

Now try to make an inference about Jacob. Do you think Jacob cares about how he looks?

Inference: Jacob _____

_____

• Look at all the facts in the story. Jacob hadn't combed his hair. He hadn't washed his face. His shirt was wrinkled. One shoelace was not tied.

• Now go beyond what you've read. What can you guess about Jacob? Your inference will come from what you read and what you already know. Did you guess that Jacob doesn't care about how he looks? You can infer that because Jacob hadn't combed his hair or washed his face. Also, his shirt was wrinkled, and his shoelace was not tied.

Name _____   Date _____

Lesson 1

≈ **Darken the circle for the sentence that best answers the question.**

Holland is a country that is next to the sea. Dikes, or walls, are built around the towns in Holland. The walls keep the sea from flooding the towns. One day a boy saw a small hole in the dike near his town. Sea water was running out of the hole. And the hole was getting bigger. He put his finger in the hole and called for help. He waited a long time. Finally some people came to help. At last the boy could go home. He knew that the town was safe.

1. Which of these sentences is probably true?
   Ⓐ The people fixed the hole.
   Ⓑ The boy fixed the hole by himself.
   Ⓒ The people thought the boy was silly.

Shree walked to the ticket counter. She waited in line. Five other people were buying tickets. She heard people asking for seats. Some talked about left field. Others said, "One near first base." One person said, "Behind home plate."

2. Which of these sentences is probably true?
   Ⓐ Shree was going on a train trip.
   Ⓑ Shree was buying a ticket to the baseball game.
   Ⓒ Shree was in line at the movie theater.

Train tracks have signals to keep the trains from hitting each other. The train track is divided into blocks. Electricity flows through each block of track. When a train moves along the track, it runs over a switch. The switch turns on a red light. A train coming from another direction sees the red light. It stops so the two trains will not crash into each other.

3. Which of these sentences is probably true?
   Ⓐ Trains obey the signals.
   Ⓑ Red lights always mean "go."
   Ⓒ Trains always go the same way.

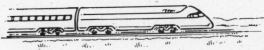

Unit 6: Inference, Lesson 1
Exploring Comprehension Skills 3, SV 9781419030918

Lesson 2

≈ **Darken the circle for the sentence that best answers the question.**

Kim gets up and goes out for the paper every morning. Then she eats breakfast and reads the comics with her mom. One day the paper stopped coming. It did not come for a week. Kim and her mom wondered what was wrong. Then Kim's mom found an envelope that was addressed to the paper. She had forgotten to mail it.

1. Which of these sentences is probably true?
   Ⓐ Kim's mom had not paid the bill for the paper.
   Ⓑ A new person was delivering the paper.
   Ⓒ Kim's mom had paid for the paper.

A drug is something that causes a change in the body. Medicines are drugs that can help parts of the body work better. Medicines can make people feel better when they are sick. But some kinds of drugs can hurt the body. Some drugs make the heart work too fast or too slow. Some drugs make people act in ways that are not safe. Certain drugs can cause death.

2. Which of these sentences is probably true?
   Ⓐ People should never use medicines.
   Ⓑ Medicines should be used with care.
   Ⓒ All medicines make people sick.

Bill got on his bike. He rode down the street past homes and trees. Then he reached the park. There he put on his shin pads and his cleats. He began kicking the round ball back and forth between his feet.

3. Which of these sentences is probably true?
   Ⓐ Bill went to play soccer.
   Ⓑ Bill went to his job after school.
   Ⓒ Bill was on an errand for his grandmother.

112

Lesson 3

≋ **Darken the circle for the sentence that best answers the question.**

Juan worked after school at a small shop. He made deliveries for the owner. One day the owner told Juan to make a delivery. Juan looked at the box. It had his address on it. Juan asked, "Is this right?" The owner told Juan to take the box to that address. When Juan got to the address, all his friends were there. They sang "Happy Birthday" to Juan.

1. Which of these sentences is probably true?
Ⓐ The owner wanted to celebrate Juan's birthday.
Ⓑ Juan didn't get along well with the owner.
Ⓒ Juan got the job through a class at school.

Cars use gasoline for fuel. When the fuel burns, a harmful gas goes into the air. The gas is carbon dioxide. A car gives off other harmful gases, too. These gases make the air all over the earth dirty. In some places, it is not safe for some people to breathe. Dirty air hurts their lungs. It can cause heart problems.

2. Which of these sentences is probably true?
Ⓐ Cars can make the air dirty.
Ⓑ Dirty air is good for your lungs.
Ⓒ Cars help clean the air.

Jim Thorpe was a star athlete. Playing sports was easy for him. He played baseball and football. He also won medals for running track at the Olympic games.

3. Which of these sentences is probably true?
Ⓐ Track is harder than baseball.
Ⓑ Baseball was Thorpe's best sport.
Ⓒ Thorpe could play more than one sport.

Bill and his dad got into the car. They were going to the store. They backed out of the driveway. Both of them heard a noise in the back of the car. As they drove, the noise got louder. The car bumped up and down. They pulled over and stopped the car. When they stepped out of the car, they noticed that it sagged to one side.

4. Which of these sentences is probably true?
Ⓐ Bill and his dad rode on a motorcycle.
Ⓑ The car was wet.
Ⓒ The car had a flat tire.

Lesson 4

≋ **Darken the circle for the sentence that best answers the question.**

Brown Bear was from an Arapaho tribe. He learned to hunt from his father. Brown Bear and his father hunted for food. His mother and sister followed them. They were gone for many days. After the hunt, the family fixed the meat of the animals they killed. They made clothes and tents from the skins of the animals. They made tools from the bones and other parts.

1. Which of these sentences is probably true?
   Ⓐ The Arapaho lived only on fish.
   Ⓑ Brown Bear taught himself to hunt.
   Ⓒ An Arapaho family worked together.

Have you heard traffic news today? It may have come from a person in a helicopter high above the city. A helicopter has blades on the top of it. It does not have wings. The blades spin fast. Then air rushes up and over the blades. The moving air pushes the helicopter straight up. When it's time to land, the helicopter can come straight down.

2. Which of these sentences is probably true?
   Ⓐ Helicopters don't fly very well.
   Ⓑ Few people ever ride in helicopters.
   Ⓒ Helicopters can land and take off in small spaces.

Look around. Do you see something made of bricks? People have built things with bricks for thousands of years. Old bricks have been found all over the world. Most bricks are made of clay. The clay is mixed with water to make a stiff mud. Then the bricks are shaped and baked. Today bricks are used to build houses. In the past, bricks were also used to make streets.

3. Which of these sentences is probably true?
   Ⓐ People do not use bricks anymore.
   Ⓑ Early Americans built many things with bricks they made.
   Ⓒ Bricks were first used on streets.

Lesson 5

≋ **Darken the circle for the sentence that best answers the question.**

May was on the road. She saw a plane over her car. It was a warm day, and the windows were rolled down. May heard the plane's engine go off and then on. This happened many times. The plane turned and came in low over the road. The plane turned again. May pulled off the road.

1. Which of these sentences is probably true?
   Ⓐ May was waiting for her mother.
   Ⓑ The plane had problems and needed to land.
   Ⓒ The pilot was counting the cars on the road.

When a ship goes from New York City to Cape Town, South Africa, it must cross the line that divides the earth. This line is called the equator. It divides north and south. When the ship crosses this line, people on the ship have a party. Everyone who is crossing this line for the first time must do tricks. When they all have had a turn, the party ends.

2. Which of these sentences is probably true?
   Ⓐ The equator is a row of cans in the ocean.
   Ⓑ A ship cannot go from New York to Cape Town.
   Ⓒ The equator is an important line.

The Tennessee River runs through high hills. For years the river flooded. Water ran over the banks of the river. The water ruined fields and houses. People built a high dam. Water collected behind the dam. This made a lake. When it rained, the floodwater went into the lake.

3. Which of these sentences is probably true?
   Ⓐ The Tennessee River dried up.
   Ⓑ Dams help stop flooding.
   Ⓒ River water is not safe to drink.

Lesson 6

≈ **Darken the circle for the sentence that best answers the question.**

All birds do not have the same kind of beaks. Some birds have short, strong beaks. These birds eat seeds. They can crack open the seeds and eat them. Some birds eat insects. These birds must have beaks that help them get to insects in the ground and inside tree trunks.

1. Which of these sentences is probably true?
   Ⓐ Birds need people to help them when they eat.
   Ⓑ Birds that eat insects need long, pointed beaks.
   Ⓒ Birds do not make good pets.

Thousands of people lived in New Orleans in 1830. All around the town were swamps. Mosquitoes lived in the swamps. People began to get sick and die. They died from a disease called yellow fever. More and more people died. It took a long time for doctors to learn that the mosquitoes gave people yellow fever.

2. Which of these sentences is probably true?
   Ⓐ Yellow fever was hard to cure.
   Ⓑ Only children got yellow fever.
   Ⓒ Doctors didn't get yellow fever.

Jazz is a kind of music. People first played jazz in America. When people play jazz, they make up the songs as they play. This makes jazz seem new all the time.

3. Which of these sentences is probably true?
   Ⓐ Jazz music is always changing.
   Ⓑ No one plays jazz today.
   Ⓒ Jazz music always stays the same.

First you need to make the ground ready. Break up the big pieces of dirt with a hoe. Use a shovel to take out all the rocks. Make sure there are no weeds or grass in the dirt. Then make straight lines in the dirt. Poke little holes in the lines. Keep the holes about one inch apart. Next put seeds in the holes.

4. Which of these sentences is probably true?
   Ⓐ This is one way to rake leaves.
   Ⓑ This tells how to make a path.
   Ⓒ This is a good way to make a garden.

Name _____   Date _____

≋ **Darken the circle for the sentence that best answers the question.**

Oil is a resource. So are coal and gas. They are fuels. We burn these fuels to make heat and power. We use gas and oil to run our cars. All three of these resources come from the earth. They were formed long before people lived on the earth.

1. Which of these sentences is probably true?
   Ⓐ No one uses resources.
   Ⓑ Oil, gas, and coal are not resources.
   Ⓒ Oil, coal, and gas help people to meet needs.

In the 1800s, a man from France wanted people all over the world to know that America stood for freedom. He asked an artist friend to help him. First the artist drew a picture of a woman wearing a long robe. He showed the woman holding a torch and wearing a crown. The man from France made a statue like the woman in the picture. The statue was finished in 1885. Now it stands on Liberty Island. It has greeted many people who have come to America.

2. Which of these sentences is probably true?
   Ⓐ The man's statue was never finished.
   Ⓑ The statue is The Statue of Liberty.
   Ⓒ The statue stands for all artists.

Even though she didn't speak, I knew Mom was mad. Her face was red. Her hands were on her hips. She was standing in the door, tapping her foot. I was late again. I tried to run up to my room fast.

3. Which of these sentences is probably true?
   Ⓐ Mom was pleased with me.
   Ⓑ People can say things without using words.
   Ⓒ Mom shouted, and I knew she was mad.

Lesson 8

≋ **Darken the circle for the sentence that best answers the question.**

How is the air heated in a hot-air balloon? Pilots use a gas flame to heat the air. If a pilot wants to go up, he or she shoots the flame up into the balloon. This makes the air hot. The pilot must cool the air to go down. Once the balloon is up, the wind guides the balloon. If there is no wind, the balloon stays in one place.

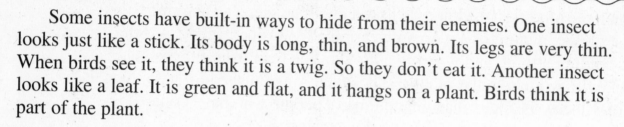

1. Which of these sentences is probably true?
   Ⓐ Hot air makes the balloon rise.
   Ⓑ Balloons get you places fast.
   Ⓒ Hot-air balloons fly with wings.

Some insects have built-in ways to hide from their enemies. One insect looks just like a stick. Its body is long, thin, and brown. Its legs are very thin. When birds see it, they think it is a twig. So they don't eat it. Another insect looks like a leaf. It is green and flat, and it hangs on a plant. Birds think it is part of the plant.

2. Which of these sentences is probably true?
   Ⓐ Birds are not very smart.
   Ⓑ Some insects are shaped like parts of plants.
   Ⓒ Insects love to play tricks.

We put all the books away in boxes. The teacher took our little bits of crayon and threw them away. She put our big ones in a box. Some children took the pictures off the walls. I washed the chalkboard. The janitor came in to lock the windows. The teacher put her plants in a box to take home.

3. Which of these sentences is probably true?
   Ⓐ It is the first day of school.
   Ⓑ It is the last day of school.
   Ⓒ There has been a fire at school.

Name _____   Date _____

≋ **Darken the circle for the sentence that best answers the question.**

Long ago, life was hard for the settlers who lived on the prairie. Often they lived far away from other people. So there wasn't much help if there was trouble. They had to make homes out of dirt because there weren't many trees. And there were always wild animals that roamed the prairie. The settlers had to raise all their own food. But sometimes it didn't rain for months, and all their crops died.

1. Which of these sentences is probably true?
   Ⓐ The settlers were brave people.
   Ⓑ The prairie was always wet and muddy.
   Ⓒ The settlers shopped for food in the East.

Jack looked up. He saw the same thing he had seen each day this week. The geese were flying south. He heard them honking as they went. "Too bad," he thought. "It will soon be cold and snowy. I'll have to play inside."

2. Which of these sentences is probably true?
   Ⓐ The geese spoke with Jack about the weather.
   Ⓑ Flying geese can mean a change of season.
   Ⓒ Jack works in a birdhouse.

Maria did not look up when the teacher spoke. She did not hear what she was supposed to do with the paper. She walked to the teacher's desk to ask. She watched the teacher's lips as he spoke. When the teacher turned his head and spoke, Maria did not hear what he said.

3. Which of these sentences is probably true?
   Ⓐ Maria needs to be a better listener.
   Ⓑ Maria cannot see the paper.
   Ⓒ Maria reads lips to understand people.

There are several ways to help a forest that is quickly losing its trees. One way is to plant young trees, or seedlings. These trees replace those that die or are cut down. And they grow quickly. Sometimes people fly over a forest and drop seeds. New trees will sprout from these seeds.

4. Which of these sentences is probably true?
   Ⓐ It is important to keep forests from dying.
   Ⓑ Trees never die in a forest.
   Ⓒ People don't really care about forests.

Exploring Comprehension Skills 3, SV 9781419030918

Lesson 10

≈ **Darken the circle for the sentence that best answers the question.**

Kate counted out five pairs of socks. She put one extra pair in the pile. She found the T-shirt she liked to sleep in. She chose some shorts and shirts. "Don't forget your teddy bear," her dad called.

1. Which of these sentences is probably true?
   Ⓐ Kate wants to see how many socks she has.
   Ⓑ Kate doesn't like nightgowns.
   Ⓒ Kate is getting ready for a trip.

Your skin is made of a thick layer of tiny, living parts called cells. Your skin helps keep you alive. It holds in the moisture that your body must have. Sometimes skin from one part of the body can be put onto another part. This is called a skin graft. Skin grafts can help someone who has had a bad burn.

2. Which of these sentences is probably true?
   Ⓐ Skin grafts don't work.
   Ⓑ Skin grows on only one part of the body.
   Ⓒ A skin graft can save a person's life.

A cave is a hole under the ground. Most caves are formed in rock called limestone. Caves are made by water. Water eats away part of the rock. Over many years, a small hole or crack in a rock becomes very big. Then it becomes a home for bears or bats. It also becomes a place people want to explore.

3. Which of these sentences is probably true?
   Ⓐ Water collects in limestone cracks.
   Ⓑ Animals stay away from caves.
   Ⓒ Caves are open to the sun.

Could you buy a candy bar today with a seashell? No. But long ago, people used seashells as money. In Africa you could buy a goat for one hundred seashells. You can still find these shells on the beach. They are about the size of a bean. But don't try to buy a candy bar with them. They're not worth a penny.

4. Which of these sentences is probably true?
   Ⓐ Long ago it was good to have many seashells.
   Ⓑ Today people shop with seashells.
   Ⓒ Wood is made from seashells.

Lesson 11

≈ **Darken the circle for the sentence that best answers the question.**

Inuit sculpture is beautiful. People come from all around to buy it. They like the simple animal shapes that the Inuits carve out of soapstone or animal bones. Inuits carve the shapes of the animals that live around them.

1. Which of these sentences is probably true?
   Ⓐ The Inuits make art from nature.
   Ⓑ You can wash with soapstone.
   Ⓒ Inuits are not good artists.

The spring was very wet. A pond formed in the field. Children playing in the field saw a duck swimming in the pond. Soon it warmed up, and the pond dried up. The duck came back to the pond with some baby ducks. But there was no water. The children brought out a plastic swimming pool. They filled the pool with water. The mother duck jumped in, but the babies could not.

2. Which of these sentences is probably true?
   Ⓐ The babies couldn't jump over the side of the pool.
   Ⓑ The mother duck didn't want the babies to swim.
   Ⓒ Many people don't like ducks.

Frank rode his horse as fast as he could. He swung his lasso above his head. The cows were running all around him. It was very dusty. Frank's dad was standing at the fence. The gate to the corral was open.

3. Which of these sentences is probably true?
   Ⓐ Frank was herding the cows to the corral.
   Ⓑ The cows needed some exercise.
   Ⓒ Frank was the winner in a horse race.

There are two kinds of rocket fuel. The oldest kind is solid. It was first made long ago by people in China. They placed it in a tube in a rocket. Then they lit it. The fuel exploded, and the rocket went up into the air. The newer fuel is a liquid. It is used more often than the solid fuel. But it works the same way. It is put in a box at the bottom of the rocket. It explodes, and the rocket goes into the air.

4. Which of these sentences is probably true?
   Ⓐ Rocket fuel has been used for a long time.
   Ⓑ A rocket costs much money to build.
   Ⓒ Rockets fly around the earth.

Name _____   Date _____

≋ **Darken the circle for the sentence that best answers the question.**

The bell rang. The boys came into the room. Some had their shirttails sticking out of their pants. Each one had a bat or a ball. All had red faces. They were glad to get into their seats. The teacher said it was time to get back to work.

1. Which of these sentences is probably true?
   Ⓐ The boys had just come in from playing.
   Ⓑ The teacher yelled at the boys.
   Ⓒ The boys had just finished math.

Lisa tore the paper off the box. She could not wait to open it. There was a wonderful brown duck inside. She placed it next to her other gifts. She already had a book and a doll. Then she and her friends ran to the table. Her dad brought in the cake.

2. Which of these sentences is probably true?
   Ⓐ Lisa had a nice birthday party.
   Ⓑ Lisa didn't like to eat cake.
   Ⓒ Lisa's mother brought in the cake.

Bill had not seen Sam all week. He rode over to Sam's house. He walked up and rang the doorbell. Sam's dad came to the door.

"Can Sam play?" asked Bill.

Sam's father said, "No. He is still in bed with a cold."

3. Which of these sentences is probably true?
   Ⓐ Bill was not able to play.
   Ⓑ Bill wanted to play football.
   Ⓒ Sam had been sick for a few days.

Lesson 13

≈ **Darken the circle for the sentence that best answers the question.**

Yeast is a tiny plant. It is mixed with sugar, flour, and warm water to make bread dough. When the dough is put in a warm place, the yeast makes it rise. The dough gets larger as it rises. After the dough rises, you must punch it down. Then you form it into a loaf and put it into the oven. The dough rises again when you bake it.

1. Which of these sentences is probably true?
   Ⓐ Yeast makes bread dough hard.
   Ⓑ Heat and yeast make bread dough rise.
   Ⓒ Brown bread does not have yeast.

Much money must be spent to keep the roads safe. In the winter, snow and ice must be plowed away. In the summer, the cracks and holes made in the roads during the winter must be fixed. Tax money is used to take care of some roads. But tax dollars are not used to fix toll roads. Money from toll roads comes from each car or truck that uses the road.

2. Which of these sentences is probably true?
   Ⓐ Most highways get money from tolls.
   Ⓑ Weather can hurt roads.
   Ⓒ Only trucks pay to use a toll road.

You don't need a friend when you play catch with a boomerang. A boomerang can come back to you when you throw it. A boomerang is a flat piece of wood. It looks like a wide *V*. The arms are shaped like two jet wings. When you throw it, air pushes up and over the arms. This keeps it in the air. If you throw it the right way, you can make it travel about half a block before it returns.

3. Which of these sentences is probably true?
   Ⓐ Boomerangs are mostly used as toys.
   Ⓑ Boomerangs can carry messages.
   Ⓒ Boomerangs need to be carried by two people.

Name _____   Date _____

Lesson 14

≈ **Darken the circle for the sentence that best answers the question.**

Steam engines were used to pull trains. Steam was made by boiling water. Water for steam was heated over a coal or wood fire. The engine carried both the water and the coal or wood. When an engine ran out of coal or wood, it had to move off the track. As engines became larger, they carried more water and more coal or wood.

1. Which of these sentences is probably true?
   Ⓐ Bigger engines needed more fuel.
   Ⓑ Steam engines are often used today.
   Ⓒ Steam engines were also used in cars.

Ben put on his best pants and shirt. His shoes were clean. His hair was neatly brushed. He and his mother went to the car. She wore a long, black skirt and a white blouse. She carried some music and a violin case. When they got to the large hall, Ben's mother told him to sit in a chair on the front row. She went to the stage.

2. Which of these sentences is probably true?
   Ⓐ Ben's mother will play music in a show.
   Ⓑ Ben didn't like music.
   Ⓒ Ben's mother always took him on rides with her.

The North and the South fought each other in the Civil War. Both sides wanted to win. The South's leader, Robert E. Lee, had a plan. He would move his whole army north. As Lee's army moved, the army from the North followed it. Both armies fought in a small town called Gettysburg. This battle lasted three days. Many men in Lee's army were hurt or killed. Lee's army could not fight anymore.

3. Which of these sentences is probably true?
   Ⓐ Lee's army won the fight.
   Ⓑ The army from the North ran away.
   Ⓒ Lee's army lost the fight.

Unit 6

Writing

≈ **Read the story. What inferences can you make? Use the clues in the story to answer the questions in complete sentences.**

The moving truck was two hours late. Aisha had hoped it would be on time. The moving man didn't have any helpers. Aisha thought he needed help. She did not see how he could do all the work. She thought about talking to the man. But she did not know what to say. The man didn't seem to be very friendly. But he hadn't done anything wrong. So Aisha waited. She needed to see how the man loaded her things. She just hoped that nothing would be broken.

1. Why has the moving truck come there?

   _____

   _____

2. Why doesn't Aisha talk to the man?

   _____

   _____

3. What kind of person is Aisha?

   _____

   _____

4. Why does Aisha seem worried?

   _____

   _____

Prewriting

≋ **Think of a time when you saw someone who was very excited, scared, or angry. What did the person do that let you know how he or she was feeling? Write a sentence that states the person's feeling in the Inference box. Write the actions that told you how the person felt in the Clue box. Then write a sentence that explains how you know about the feeling in the Prior Knowledge box.**

<table>
<tr><td>Clue
_____
_____
_____
_____</td><td>Prior Knowledge
_____
_____
_____
_____</td></tr>
</table>

Inference
_____
_____
_____
_____

On Your Own

≋ **Now use another sheet of paper to write a paragraph that tells about the feelings of the person from above. Remember, don't tell what the emotion was. Just use the clue and the prior knowledge to describe what you saw.**

ANSWER KEY

Unit 1: Facts, Assessment, p. 5
1. B
2. C
3. B
4. B

Unit 2: Sequence, Assessment, p. 6
1. 2, 1
2. A

Unit 3: Context, Assessment, p. 7
1. B
2. A
3. B
4. A

Unit 4: Main Idea, Assessment, p. 8
1. A
2. A
3. C
4. B

Unit 5: Conclusion, Assessment, p. 9
1. C
2. A
3. A

Unit 6: Inference, Assessment, p. 10
1. A
2. A
3. A
4. B

Unit 1: Facts
Lesson 1, pp. 13–14
1. A   5. A
2. C   6. C
3. C   7. B
4. C   8. A

Lesson 2, pp. 15–16
1. B   5. C
2. A   6. B
3. A   7. B
4. B   8. C

Lesson 3, pp. 17–18
1. C   5. A
2. C   6. C
3. C   7. B
4. B   8. A

Lesson 4, pp. 19–20
1. C   5. C
2. C   6. B
3. B   7. A
4. A   8. C

Lesson 5, pp. 21–22
1. C   5. C
2. B   6. B
3. B   7. C
4. A   8. B

Lesson 6, pp. 23–24
1. C   5. A
2. A   6. C
3. B   7. B
4. C   8. B

Lesson 7, pp. 25–26
1. B   5. A
2. A   6. C
3. C   7. C
4. B   8. C

Lesson 8, pp. 27–28
1. C   5. A
2. C   6. C
3. C   7. B
4. B   8. A

Writing, pp. 29–30
Possible answers:
1. Humans have traveled there and brought back soil to study.
2. The soil is made of rock and glass.
3. Each glass bit is about as small as a period.
Prewriting: Check students' answers.

Unit 2: Sequence
Lesson 1, p. 34
1. 1, 2   3. A
2. C   4. B

Lesson 2, p. 36
1. 2, 1   3. C
2. A   4. C

Lesson 3, p. 38
1. 2, 1   3. C
2. A   4. B

Lesson 4, p. 40
1. 2, 1   3. C
2. C   4. B

Lesson 5, p. 42
1. 1, 2   3. A
2. C   4. B

Lesson 6, p. 44
1. 2, 1   3. B
2. A   4. C

Lesson 7, p. 46
1. 2, 1   3. A
2. B   4. C

Lesson 8, p. 48
1. 2, 1   3. A
2. C   4. C

Writing, pp. 49–50
Possible answers:
1. Julio took the clay out of the bag.
2. He shaped it into a bowl.
3. He let it dry.
Prewriting: Check students' sequence and use of time order words.

Unit 3: Context
Lesson 1, p. 53
1. C   3. B
2. A   4. A

Lesson 2, p. 54
1. C   3. C
2. A   4. B

Lesson 3, p. 55
1. C   3. C
2. B   4. A

Lesson 4, p. 56
1. A   3. A
2. C   4. B

Lesson 5, p. 57
1. C   3. A
2. B   4. C

Lesson 6, p. 58
1. B   3. C
2. C   4. B

Lesson 7, p. 59
1. A   3. B
2. C   4. B

Lesson 8, p. 60
1. B   3. C
2. B   4. A

Lesson 9, p. 61
1. A   3. C
2. B   4. A

Lesson 10, p. 62
1. A   3. B
2. C   4. C

Lesson 11, p. 63
1. C   3. C
2. B   4. B

Lesson 12, p. 64
1. C   3. A
2. B   4. C

Lesson 13, p. 65
1. C   3. C
2. B   4. B

Lesson 14, p. 66
1. A   3. A
2. C   4. B

Lesson 15, p. 67
1. C   3. A
2. B   4. B

Lesson 16, p. 68
1. B   3. C
2. A   4. A

Writing, pp. 69–70
1. afternoon   4. glass
2. leaves   5. joke
3. feed
For 6–9, answers will vary.
Prewriting: Check students' graphic organizers and paragraphs for the use of context clues.

Unit 4: Main Idea
Lesson 1, p. 73
1. A
2. B
3. A

Lesson 2, p. 74
1. B   3. A
2. A   4. C

Lesson 3, p. 75
1. B   3. B
2. A   4. C

Lesson 4, p. 76
1. B   3. C
2. C   4. A

Lesson 5, p. 77
1. B   3. B
2. A   4. C

Lesson 6, p. 78
1. A
2. B
3. C

Lesson 7, p. 79
1. C   3. B
2. A   4. B

Lesson 8, p. 80
1. B   3. C
2. A   4. C

Lesson 9, p. 81
1. B   3. C
2. B   4. A

Lesson 10, p. 82
1. B
2. B
3. C

Lesson 11, p. 83
1. A
2. A
3. B

Lesson 12, p. 84
1. B   3. A
2. A   4. B

Answer Key
Exploring Comprehension Skills 3, SV 9781419030918

Lesson 13, p. 85
1. C   3. B
2. A   4. C

Lesson 14, p. 86
1. C   3. B
2. A   4. B

Lesson 15, p. 87
1. A
2. C
3. A

Lesson 16, p. 88
1. A   3. C
2. C   4. B

Writing, pp. 89–90
1. Not all presidents lived in the White House.
2. There is little land to farm in Japan, so many kinds of food are shipped in.
3. Paul Bunyan's footsteps helped make lakes.
Prewriting: Check students' main idea and details.

Unit 5: Conclusion
Lesson 1, p. 93
1. A   3. B
2. B   4. C

Lesson 2, p. 94
1. A
2. B
3. C

Lesson 3, p. 95
1. A
2. C
3. C

Lesson 4, p. 96
1. B
2. B
3. C

Lesson 5, p. 97
1. A
2. C
3. A

Lesson 6, p. 98
1. C
2. B
3. C

Lesson 7, p. 99
1. B
2. C
3. B

Lesson 8, p. 100
1. A
2. C
3. B

Lesson 9, p. 101
1. C
2. A
3. B

Lesson 10, p. 102
1. A
2. B
3. C

Lesson 11, p. 103
1. B
2. A
3. C

Lesson 12, p. 104
1. C
2. B
3. A

Lesson 13, p. 105
1. C
2. A
3. B

Lesson 14, p. 106
1. A
2. A
3. A

Writing, pp. 107–108
1. Aunt Lynn did not live with Ann. They visited each other often.
2. Aunt Lynn's eyes were not always weak. She could read to Ann.
3. Ann makes Aunt Lynn happy. She visits her and reads to her.
Prewriting: Check students' clues and conclusion.

Unit 6: Inference
Lesson 1, p. 111
1. A
2. B
3. A

Lesson 2, p. 112
1. A
2. B
3. A

Lesson 3, p. 113
1. A   3. C
2. A   4. C

Lesson 4, p. 114
1. C
2. C
3. B

Lesson 5, p. 115
1. B
2. C
3. B

Lesson 6, p. 116
1. B   3. A
2. A   4. C

Lesson 7, p. 117
1. C
2. B
3. B

Lesson 8, p. 118
1. A
2. B
3. B

Lesson 9, p. 119
1. A   3. C
2. B   4. A

Lesson 10, p. 120
1. C   3. A
2. C   4. A

Lesson 11, p. 121
1. A   3. A
2. A   4. A

Lesson 12, p. 122
1. A
2. A
3. C

Lesson 13, p. 123
1. B
2. B
3. A

Lesson 14, p. 124
1. A
2. A
3. C

Writing, pp. 125–126
1. Aisha is moving.
2. Aisha doesn't want to talk to the man because he doesn't seem friendly. She wants to give the man a chance. She wants to see if the man knows what he is doing.
3. Aisha is careful, shy, and worries about things.
Prewriting: Check students' clue, prior knowledge, and inference.

Exploring Comprehension Skills 3, SV 9781419030918